For Grades 6–8

Literature
FOR EVERY
LEARNER

Differentiating Instruction With Menus for Poetry, Short Stories, and Novels

For Grades 6–8

Literature
FOR EVERY
LEARNER

Differentiating Instruction With Menus for Poetry, Short Stories, and Novels

Laurie E. Westphal

PRUFROCK PRESS INC.
WACO, TEXAS

Edited by Lacy Compton

Layout and cover design by Raquel Trevino

ISBN-13: 978-1-61821-140-8

Prufrock Press Inc.
P.O. Box 8813
Waco, TX 76714-8813
Phone: (800) 998-2208
Fax: (800) 240-0333
http://www.prufrock.com

TABLE OF CONTENTS

CHAPTER 1

Choice

Choice in the Secondary Classroom

When considering choice in the secondary classroom, we must first picture our classrooms and our curricula, including the wide range of abilities we may find within a single classroom, even one designated as Pre-AP or AP. It has become increasing more popular to implement an inclusive, open door, mixed-ability model. Teachers may find that their one classroom contains special needs students, on-level students, bilingual/ESL students, and gifted students, all wanting to be successful, all with different needs. Cipani (1995) stated it best in his assessment of the variety of needs found in these "inclusive" classrooms:

Students who are academically gifted, those who have had abundant experiences, and those who have demonstrated proficiency with lesson content typically tend to perform well when instruction is anchored at the "implicit" end of the instructional continuum. In contrast, low-performing students (i.e., students at risk for school failure, students with learning disabilities, and students with other special needs) and students with limited experience or proficiency with lesson content are most successful when instruction is explicit. Students with average academic performance tend to benefit most from the use of a variety of instructional methods that address individual needs. Instructional decisions for most students, therefore, should be based on assessment of individual needs. (pp. 498–499)

Acknowledging that these varied and often contradictory needs arise within a mixed-ability setting can lead to frustration, especially when trying to design one assignment or task that can fit everyone's needs. There are few if any traditional, teacher-directed lessons that can be implicit, explicit, and based on individual needs all at the same time. There is, however, one *technique* that tries to accomplish this: the implementation of choice.

Choice: The Superman of Techniques?

Can the offering of appropriate choices really be the hero when our classrooms have such diversity of abilities? Can it leap buildings in a single bound and meet the needs of our implicit, explicit, and individual interests? If introduced properly, certainly it can. By considering the use and subsequent benefits of choice, it becomes apparent that by offering choices, teachers really can meet the needs of the range of students in such a diverse classroom setting. Ask adults whether they would prefer to choose what to do or be told what to do, and of course, they are going to say they would prefer to have a choice. Students have these same feelings. Students will make choices based on their needs, which makes everyone involved in the classroom experience a little less stressed and frustrated.

Why Is Choice Important to Middle School Students?

" . . . Almost every kid in middle school wants freedom of his or her choice of what they want to work on. They just do."

—Eighth-grade student

First, we have to consider who (or what) our middle school students personify. During these years, adolescents struggle to determine who they are and how they fit into the world around them. They constantly try new ideas (the hydrogen peroxide in the hair sounded like a good idea at the time), new experiences ("If you sit on the second-floor roof of your home one more time, I will tell your parents!"), and a flux of personalities (preppy one day, dark nails and lipstick the next) in order to obtain "zen" and find themselves. During this process, which can take from a few months to a few years depending on the child, academics are not always at the forefront of his mind unless the student has chosen that as part of his identity. Knowing this, instruction and higher level products have to engage the individuals these students are trying to become; implementing choice as a way to engage these students has many explicit benefits once it has been developed as the center of high-level thinking.

"I like being able to choose, because I can pick what I am good at and avoid my weaknesses."

—Eighth-grade student

One benefit of choice is its ability to meet the needs of so many different students and their learning styles. Although choice is appropriate for all ability levels, it is especially well received by advanced and gifted students. The Dunedin College of Education (Keen, 2001) conducted a research study on the preferred learning styles and techniques of 250 gifted students. Students were asked to rank different learning options; of the 13 different options described to the students, only one option did not receive at least one negative response. It was the option of having choices. All students may have different learning styles and preferences, yet choice is the one option that meets all students' needs. Unlike elementary students, middle school students have been engaged in the learning process long enough that they usually can recognize their own strengths and weaknesses, as well their learning styles. By allowing choice, students are able to choose what best fits their learning styles and educational needs.

> *". . . I am different in the way I do stuff. I like to build stuff with my hands more than other things."*
>
> **—Sixth-grade student**

Another benefit of choice is a greater sense of independence for the students, as some of them have not had the opportunity to consider their own learning in the past. What a powerful feeling! Students will have the opportunity to design and create products based on their own vision, rather than what their teacher envisions for them. When using choice, there is a possibility for more than one "right" product; everyone can make the task he or she has selected his or her own, no matter his or her level of ability. When students would enter my secondary classroom, they often had been trained by previous teachers to produce exactly what the teacher wanted, not what the students thought would be best. Teaching my students that what they envision could be correct (and incredible) was often a struggle. "Is this what you want?" or "Is this right?" were popular questions as we started the school year. After being offered various choice opportunities and experiencing the success that often accompanies their producing quality products that they envision, the students begin to take the responsibility for their work. Allowing students to have choices in the products they create to show their learning helps create independence at any age, or within any ability level.

> *"It [choice] puts me in a good mood to participate!"*
>
> **—Seventh-grade student**

Strengthened student focus on the required content is a third benefit. Middle school students already have begun to transition from an academic focus to more of a social one. Choice is a way to help bring their focus back to the academic aspect of school. When students have choices in the activities they wish to complete, they are more focused on the learning that leads to their choice product. Students become excited when they learn information that can help them develop a product they would like to create. This excitement can manifest in thought-provoking questions and discussions during a class rather than just hurrying through instruction so they can get to the homework. Students will pay close attention to instruction and have an immediate application for the knowledge being presented in class. Also, if students are focused, they are less likely to be off task during instruction.

The final benefit (and I am sure there are many more), is the simple fact that by offering varied choices at appropriate levels, implicit instructional options (and their counterpart, explicit instructional options) as well as individual needs can be addressed without anyone getting overly frustrated or overworked. Many a great educator has referred to the idea that the best learning takes place when the students have a desire to learn and can feel successful during the process. Some secondary students have a desire to be taught information, others prefer to explore and learn things that is new to them; still others do not want to learn anything unless it is of interest to them. By incorporating different activities from which to choose, students can stretch beyond what they already know, and teachers can create a void that needs to be filled in order for students to complete a product they have selected for themselves. This void leads to a desire to learn.

A Point to Ponder: Making Good Choices Is a Skill

"Even if my students know how to make choices already, I can certainly reinforce the process."

—Secondary teacher

When we consider making good choices as a skill, much like writing an effective paragraph, it becomes easy enough to understand the processes needed to encourage students to make their own choices. In keeping with this analogy, students could certainly figure out how to write on their own, perhaps even how to compose sentences and paragraphs by modeling other examples. Imagine, however, the progress and strength of the writing produced when students are given guidance and even the most basic of instruction on how to accomplish the task. Even with instruction from the teacher, the written piece is still their own, but the quality of the finished piece is so much stronger when guidance is provided during the process. The same is true with the quality of choices students can make when it comes to their instruction and showing their level of knowledge in the classroom.

As with writing, students could make their own choices; however, when the teacher provides background knowledge and assistance, the choices become more meaningful and the products a student chooses to create become richer. Certainly all students need guidance in the choice-making process, but sometimes our on-level and special needs students may need the most help; they may not have been in an educational setting that has allowed them to experience different products and the idea of choice can be new to them. Some students may only have experienced basic instructional choices like choosing between two journal prompts or perhaps the option of making a poster or a PowerPoint about the content being studied. Other students may not have experienced even this level of choice. This can cause frustration for both teacher and student.

Teaching Choices as a Skill

So what is the best way to provide this guidance and develop the skill of making good choices? First, select the appropriate number of choices for your students. Although the goal may be to have students choose between 12 different options, teachers might start by having their students choose between three predetermined choices the first day (if they were using a meal menu, students might choose a breakfast activity). Then, after those products have been created and submitted for grading, students can choose between another three options a few days later, and again another three perhaps the following week. By breaking the choices into smaller manageable pieces, teachers are reinforcing how to approach a more complex and/or varied situation that involves choice in the future. All students can work up to making complex choices with longer lists of options as their choice skill-level increases.

Second, although middle school students crave their independence, they may still need guidance on how to select the option that is best for them. They may not automatically gravitate toward varied options without an excited and detailed description of each choice. For the most part, students have been trained to produce what the teacher requests, which means that when given a choice, they will usually try to ferret out what the teacher wants them to produce. That means that when the teacher discusses the different menu options, she will need to be equally as excited about each. The discussion of the different choices has to be animated and specific. For example, if the content is all very similar, the focus would be on the product: "If you want to do some singing, this one is for you!" or "If you want to write and draw, mark this one as a maybe!" Sometimes, choices may differ based on both content and product, in which case, both can be pointed out to students to assist them in making a good choice. "You have some different choices for this story's menu, if you would like work with creating new endings as well as drawing, check this one as a maybe. If you are thinking you want to act and work with the characters, this one might be for you!" This thinking aloud or teacher feedback helps the students begin to see how they might approach different choices. The more exposure they have to the processing the teacher provides, the more skillful they become in their choice making.

How Can Teachers Provide Choices?

When people go to a restaurant, the common goal is to find something on the menu to satisfy their hunger. Students come into our classrooms having a hunger as well—a hunger for learning. Choice menus are a way of allowing our students to choose how they would like to satisfy that intellectual hunger. At the very least, a menu is a list of choices that students use to select an activity (or activities) they would like to complete in order to show what they have learned. At best, it is a complex system in which a student earns points toward a goal determined by the teacher or the student. The points are assigned to products based on the different levels of Bloom's revised taxonomy and the choices may come from different areas of study. If possible, a menu should also incorporate a free-choice option for those "picky eaters" who would like to make a special order to satisfy their needs.

The next few sections provide examples of different menu formats that will be used in this book. Each menu has its own benefits, limitations or drawbacks, and time considerations. An explanation of the free-choice option and its management will follow the information on each type of menu.

Meal Menu

Description

The Meal menu (see Figure 1.1) is a menu with a total of at least nine predetermined choices as well as two or more enrichment/optional activities for students. The choices are created at the various levels of Bloom's revised taxonomy (Anderson & Krathwohl, 2001) and incorporate different learning styles, with the levels getting progressively higher and more complex as students progress from breakfast to lunch and then to dinner. All products carry the same weight for grading and have similar expectations for completion time and effort. The enrichment or optional (dessert) options can be used for extra credit or can replace another meal option at the teacher's discretion.

Benefits

Great starter menu. This menu is very straightforward and easy to understand, so time is saved in presenting the completion expectations.

Flexibility. This menu can cover either one topic in depth or three different objectives or aspects within a topic, with each meal representing a different aspect. With this menu, students have the option of completing three products: one from each meal.

Optional enrichment. Although not required, the dessert category of the meal menu allows students to have the option of going further or deeper if time during the unit permits.

Chunkability. The meal menu is very easy to break apart into smaller pieces. Whether you have students who need support in making choices or you only want to focus on one aspect of a story at a time, this menu can accommodate these decisions. Students could be asked to select a breakfast while the rest of the menu is put on hold until the breakfast product is submitted, then a lunch product is selected, and so on.

Friendly design. Students quickly understand how to use this menu because of its real-world application.

Weighting. All products are equally weighted, so recording grades and maintaining paperwork are easily accomplished with this menu.

Short time period. This menu is intended for shorter periods of time, between 1–3 weeks.

Figure 1.1. Meal menu.

Limitations

None.

Time Considerations

The meal menu is usually intended for shorter amounts of completion time—at the most, it should take 3 weeks with students working outside of class and submitting one product each week. If a menu focuses on one topic in-depth and the students have time in class to work on their products, the menu could be completed in one week.

Poetry Shape Menu

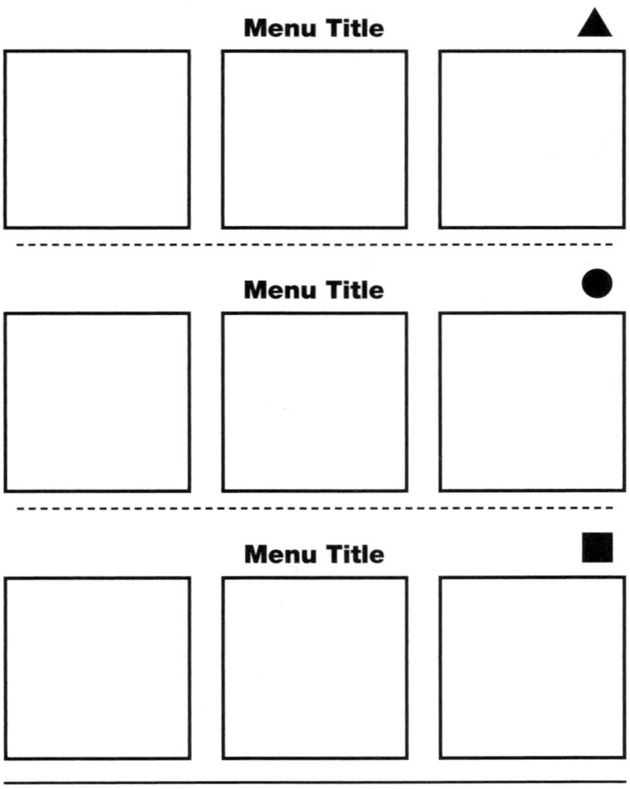

Description

The Poetry Shape menu (see Figure 1.2) is a menu that has been specifically designed for poems. Its format is unique as it allows teachers to determine whether to provide three, six, or nine choices for their students. The number of choices are often determined by the amount of time the teacher plans to spend with the study of the work. The choices are created at the various levels of Bloom's revised taxonomy (Anderson & Krathwohl, 2001) and incorporate different learning styles. All products within the same row carry the same weight for grading and have similar expectations for completion time and effort.

Menu Title ▲

Menu Title ●

Menu Title ■

Figure 1.2. Poetry Shape menu.

Benefits

Flexibility. This menu offers the opportunity for students to create one, two, or three products based on the amount of time spent on the study of the poem. If the teacher only has time for students to create one product, he may give students a strip of choices (triangle, circle, square), which have been tiered based on modifications

Friendly design. Students quickly understand how to use this menu. It is easy to explain how to make the choices based on the divisions located on the page.

Weighting. All products are equally weighted, so recording grades and maintaining paperwork are easily accomplished with this menu.

Short time period. This menu is intended for a short period of time, at most one week.

Limitations

None.

Time Considerations

This menu is usually intended for a short amount of completion time, based on the amount of time spent on the poem—at the most, it should take one week. If the teacher chooses to provide students with a single tiered ability strip, it could be completed in one or two class periods.

Tic-Tac-Toe Menu

> *"They [Tic-Tac-Toe menus] can be a real pain. A lot of times I only liked two of the choices and had to do the last one. Usually I got stuck with a play or presentation."*
>
> —Sixth-grade math student (asked to step out of her comfort zone based on the tic-tac-toe design)

Description

The Tic-Tac-Toe menu (see Figure 1.3) is a well-known, commonly used menu that contains a total of eight predetermined choices and, if appropriate, one free choice for students. Choices can be created at the same level of Bloom's revised taxonomy (Anderson & Krathwohl, 2001), or be arranged in such a way as to allow for the three different levels or even three different content areas. If all of the choices have been created at the same level of Bloom's revised taxonomy, each choice carries the same weight for grading and has similar expectations for completion time and effort.

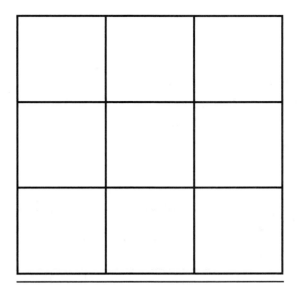

Figure 1.3. Tic-Tac-Toe menu.

Benefits

Flexibility. This menu can cover one topic in depth, or three different topics, objectives, or even content areas. When this menu covers just one objective and all tasks are from the same level of Bloom's revised taxonomy, students have the option of completing three projects in a tic-tac-toe pattern, or simply picking three from the menu. When it covers three objectives or different levels of Bloom's revised taxonomy, students will need to complete a tic-tac-toe pattern (either a vertical column or horizontal row) to be sure they have completed one activity from each objective or level.

Stretching. When students make choices on this menu completing a row or column, based on its design, they will usually face one choice that is out of their comfort zone, be it through its level of Bloom's revised taxonomy, product learning style, or content. They will complete this "uncomfortable" choice because they want to do the other two options in that row or column.

Friendly design. Students quickly understand how to use this menu. It is nonthreatening because it does not contain points, and therefore seems to encourage students to stretch out of their comfort zone.

Weighting. All projects are equally weighted, so recording grades and maintaining paperwork are easily accomplished with this menu.

Short time period. This menu is intended for shorter periods of time, between 1–3 weeks.

Limitations

Few topics. This menu only covers one or three topics.

Student compromise. Although this menu does allow for choice, a student will sometimes have to compromise and complete an activity he or she would not have chosen because it completes the required tic-tac-toe. (This is not always bad, though!)

Time Considerations

This menu is usually intended for shorter amounts of completion time—at the most, this menu should take 3 weeks with one product submitted each week. If a Tic-Tac-Toe menu focuses on one topic in-depth and the students have time in class to work on their products, the menu could be completed in one week.

List Menu

"I like that you can add up the points to be over 100, so even if you make some small mistakes, your grade could still be a 100."

—Seventh-grade student, when asked how he felt about a recent List menu

Description

The List menu (see Figure 1.4), or Challenge List, has a total of at least 10 predetermined choices, each with its own point value, and at least one free choice for students. Choices are simply listed with assigned points based on the levels of Bloom's revised taxonomy (Anderson & Krathwohl, 2001). The choices carry different weights and have different expectations for completion time and effort. A point criterion is set forth that equals 100%, and students choose how they wish to attain that point goal. There are two versions of the List menu included in this book: the Challenge List (one topic in depth) and the Three-Topic List menu (which based on its structure can accommodate multiple topics).

Benefits

Responsibility. Students have complete control over their grades. They really like the idea that they can guarantee their grades if they complete their required work and meet the expectations set forth in the rubric. If students do not earn full credit on one of the chosen products, they can complete another to be sure they have met their goal. This responsibility over their own grades also allows a shift in thinking about grades—whereas students may think of grades in terms of how the teacher judged their work, or what the teacher gave them, having control over their grades leads students to understand that they earn their grades.

Different learning levels. This menu also has the flexibility to allow for individualized contracts for different learning levels within the classroom. Because there can be many ability levels within a classroom, it may be necessary to contract students based on their ability or even results from the pretesting of content, in which case, each student can contract for a certain number of points for his or her 100%.

Figure 1.4. List menu.

Concept reinforcement. This menu also allows for an in-depth study of material; however, with the different levels of Bloom's revised taxonomy being represented, students who are still learning the concepts can choose some of the lower level point value products to reinforce the basics before jumping into the higher-level activities.

Variety. A List menu offers a larger variety of product choices. There is guaranteed to be a product of interest to everyone. (And if there isn't, there is always free choice!)

Limitations

One topic. This menu is best used for one topic in depth, so that students don't miss any specific content.

Preparation. Teachers need to have all materials ready at the beginning of the unit for students to be able to choose any of the activities on the list, which requires advanced planning.

Time Considerations

The List menu is usually intended for shorter amounts of completion time—at the most, 2 weeks. (*Note*: Once the materials are assembled, the preparation is minimal!)

2-5-8 or 20-50-80 Menu

"My least favorite menu is 2-5-8. You can't just do the easy ones. If you pick a 2, then you gotta do an 8, or you have to do two 5s. I don't think you should do any more of these. No matter what, you had to do one of the hard ones."

—Seventh-grade student

Description

A 2-5-8 menu (see Figure 1.5), or 20-50-80 menu, has two variations; one in which activities are worth 2, 5, or 8 points, and one in which the activities are worth 20, 50, or 80. The 20, 50, and 80 version often is easier to grade with a rubric based on 5s (like the one included in this book). Both are variations on a List menu, with a total of at least eight predetermined choices: at least two choices with a point value of 2 (20), at least four choices with a point value of 5

(50), and at least two choices with a point value of 8 (80). Choices are assigned points based on the levels of Bloom's revised taxonomy (Anderson & Krathwohl, 2001). Choices with a point value of 2 represent the remember and understand levels, choices with a point value of 5 represent the apply and analyze levels, and choices with a point value of 8 represent the evaluate and create levels. All levels of choices carry different weights and have different expectations for completion time and effort. Students are expected to earn 10 (100) points for a 100%. Students choose what combination they would like to use to attain that point goal.

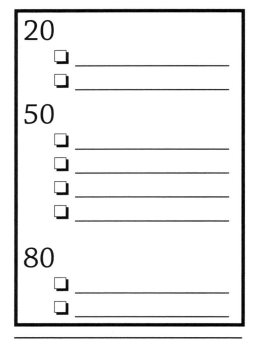

Figure 1.5. 20-50-80 menu.

Benefits

Responsibility. With this menu, students have complete control over their grades.

Low stress. This menu is one of the shortest menus and if students choose well, only requires students to complete two products. This menu is usually not as daunting as some of the longer, more complex menus. It provides students a great introduction into the process of making choices.

Guaranteed activity. This menu's design is also set up in such a way that students must complete at least one activity at a higher level of Bloom's revised taxonomy in order to reach their point goal.

Limitations

One topic. This menu works best with in-depth study of one topic.

Higher level thinking. Students usually choose to complete only one activity at a higher level of thinking.

Time Considerations

The 2-5-8 menu is usually intended for a shorter amount of completion time—at the most, one week.

Free Choice in the Mixed-Ability Classroom

"I don't know if I really liked it at first. It's a lot easier to just do the basic stuff and get it over with but when Mrs. [teacher] told us she wanted us to submit at least one free choice, I really got into it! I mean, I could do something I wanted to do? How often do you get to do THAT in school?"

—Eighth-grade GT student

Most of the menus included in this book allow students to submit a free choice as a product. This free choice is a product of their choosing that addresses the content being studied and shows what the student has learned about the topic. Although this option is offered, students may not fully understand its benefits or immediately respond to the opportunity even after it has been explained. Although certain students may have experienced choice before and may be very excited by the idea of taking charge of their own learning, other students, especially those with special needs, may not have had much exposure to this concept. Their educational experiences tend to be objective based and teacher driven. This is not to say that these students would not respond well to the idea of free choice; in fact, they can embrace it as enthusiastically as gifted students. The most significant difference between these two groups successfully approaching free choice is the amount of content needed by the student before he or she embarks on the proposed option. Special needs students need to feel confident in their knowledge of the content and information before they are ready to step out on their own, propose their own idea, and create their unique product.

The menus in this book that include a free choice option require that students submit a free choice proposal form for their teacher's consideration. Figure 1.6 shows two sample proposal forms that have been used many times successfully in my mixed-ability classroom. With middle school students, this cuts down greatly on the whining that often accompanies any task given to students. The form used is based on the type of menu being presented. If students are using the Tic-Tac-Toe, Meal, or Meal menu, there is no need to submit a point proposal form. A copy of these forms should be provided to each student when a menu is first introduced. A discussion should be held with the students so they understand the expectations of a free choice. I always have a few students who do not want to complete a task on the menu; they are welcome to create their own free choice and submit it for approval. The biggest complainers will not always go to the trouble to complete the form and have it approved, but it is their choice not to

Name: _____ Teacher's Approval: _____

Free-Choice Proposal Form for Point-Based Menu

Points Requested: _____ Points Approved: _____

<u>Proposal Outline</u>

1. What specific topic or idea will you learn about?

2. What criteria should be used to grade it? (Neatness, content, creativity, artistic value, etc.)

3. What will your product look like?

4. What materials will you need from the teacher to create this product?

Name: _____ Teacher's Approval: _____

Free-Choice Proposal Form

<u>Proposal Outline</u>

1. What specific topic or idea will you learn about?

2. What criteria should be used to grade it? (Neatness, content, creativity, artistic value, etc.)

3. What will your product look like?

4. What materials will you need from the teacher to create this product?

Figure 1.6. Sample proposal forms for free choice.

do so. The more free choice is used and encouraged, the more students will begin to request it. How the students show their knowledge will begin to shift from teacher-focused to student-designed activities. If students do not want to make a proposal using the proposal form after the teacher has discussed the entire menu and its activities, they can place the unused form in a designated place in the classroom. Other students may want to use their form, and it is often surprising who wants to submit a proposal form after hearing about the opportunity!

Proposal forms must be submitted before students begin working on their free-choice products. The teacher then knows what the student should be working on and the student knows the expectations the teacher has for that product. Once approved, the forms can easily be stapled to the student's menu sheet for reference during the creation and grading process. The student can refer to it as he or she develops his or her free-choice product, and when the grading takes place, the teacher can refer to the proposed agreement for the "graded" features of the product.

Each part of the proposal form is important and needs to be discussed with students:

- *Name/Teacher's Approval.* The student must submit this form to the teacher for approval. The teacher will carefully review all of the information, discuss any suggestions or alterations with the student, if needed, and then sign the top.
- *Points Requested.* Found only on the point-based menu proposal form, this is where negotiation may need to take place. Students usually will submit their first request for a very high number (even the 100% goal). They tend to equate the amount of time a product will take with the amount of points it should earn. Please note, however, that the points are always based on the levels of Bloom's revised taxonomy. For example, a PowerPoint presentation with a vocabulary word quiz would get minimal points, although it may have taken a long time to create. If the students have not been exposed to the levels of Bloom's revised taxonomy, this can be difficult to explain. You can always refer to the popular "Bloom's verbs" to help explain the difference between time requirements and higher level activities.
- *Points Approved.* Found only on the point-based menu proposal form, this is the final decision recorded by the teacher once the point haggling is finished.
- *Proposal Outline.* This is where the student will tell you everything about the product he or she intends to complete. These questions should be completed in such a way that you can really picture what the student is planning on creating. This also shows you that the student has thought out what he or she wants to create.

o   *What specific topic or idea will you learn about?* Students need to be specific here. It is not acceptable to just write "reading" or the title of the novel, story, or poem. This is where they look at the objectives or standards of the unit and choose which one their product demonstrates.

o   *What criteria should be used to grade it?* Although there are guidelines for most of the products that the students might create, it is important for the students to explain what criteria are most important to evaluate the product. The student may indicate that the guidelines being used for the predetermined project is fine; however, he or she may also want to add other criteria here.

o   *What will your product look like?* It is important that this be as detailed as possible. If a student cannot express what it will "look like," then he or she has probably not given the free-choice plan enough thought.

o   *What materials will you need from the teacher to create this product?* This is an important consideration. Sometimes students do not have the means to purchase items for their project. This can be negotiated, as well, but if you ask what students may need, then they often will develop even grander ideas for their free choice.

CHAPTER 2

How to Use Menus in the Classroom

There are different ways to use instructional menus in the classroom. In order to decide how to implement a menu, the following questions should be considered:

- How much prior knowledge of the topic being taught do the students have before the unit or lesson begins?
- How confident are your students in making choices and working independently?
- How much intellectually appropriate information is readily available for students to obtain on their own?

After considering these questions, it becomes easier to determine how menus can be best implemented.

Building Background Knowledge or Accessing Prior Knowledge

> *"I have students with so many different experiences—sometimes I spend more time than I allotted to review and get everyone up to speed before we get started."*
>
> —Social studies teacher

There are many ways to use menus in the classroom. One way that is often overlooked is using menus to access or build background knowledge before a unit begins. This is frequently used when students have had exposure to upcoming content in the past, perhaps during the previous year's instruction, or through similar life experiences. Although they may have been exposed to the content previously, students may not remember the content details at the level needed to proceed with this year's instruction immediately. A shorter menu (the 20-50-80 menu is great for this) covering the previous years' objectives can be provided during the week prior to the new unit so students have the opportunity to recall and engage the information in a meaningful way before they are put on the spot to use it. Students are then ready to take it to a deeper level during this year's unit. For example, a week before starting a unit on *The Diary of Anne Frank*, the teacher may use a short menu on World War II, knowing that the students may have had the content in the past and should be able to successfully work independently on the menu by engaging their prior knowledge. By offering a menu on the events of the war, students will have a greater understanding of the events in the novel, and very little class time was taken for the prenovel background work. Students can work on products from the menu as anchor activities and homework throughout the week prior to the Anne Frank unit, with all products being submitted prior to its initiation. The students have been working independently on the topic for at least one week and are ready to begin the novel.

Enrichment and Supplemental Activities

"I have some students who are always finishing early. I hate to just have them read ahead or do more questions since they end up finishing the novel before everyone else, which can cause its own set of frustrations."

—Reading teacher

Integrating menus into instruction for enrichment and as supplementary activities are the most common uses for menus in the classroom. In this case, the students usually do not have a lot of background knowledge and the intellectually appropriate information about the topic may not be readily available to all students. The teacher will introduce the menu and the activities at the beginning of a unit. The teacher will then progress through the necessary content at the normal rate, using his or her own curricular materials and periodically allowing class time and homework time throughout the unit for students to work on their menu choices to supplement a deeper understanding of the information being presented. This method is very effective, as it builds in an immediate use for the information the teacher is covering. For example, at the beginning of a novel unit on *Dragonwings*, the teacher many introduce the menu with the explanation that students may have not read enough of the novel to complete all of their choices yet. During the unit, however, as they read further, they will be prepared to work on the choices in which they are interested. If students want to work ahead, they certainly can read ahead of the class, but that is not required. Although gifted students often see this as a challenge and will begin to tear through a novel before the teacher discusses each chapter, special needs students begin to develop questions about upcoming events and are ready to ask when the class gets to that point in the novel. As teachers, we often fight the battle of having students read ahead or "come to class prepared to discuss and question." By introducing a menu at the beginning of a novel and allowing students to complete products as reading progresses, the students naturally begin looking forward and come to class prepared without it being a completely separate requirement.

Mainstream Instructional Activities

> *"I really wanted to be able to use reading groups but that just isn't really done in middle school. I used a menu for my class work and it allowed me to bring in some much needed reading group support."*
>
> —Eighth-grade language arts teacher

Another option for using menus and choice in the classroom is to replace certain whole-class curricular activities the teacher uses to teach specific aspects of a novel. In this case, the students may have some limited background knowledge about the literary elements and information is readily available for them in their classroom resources. The teacher would pick and choose which aspects must be directly taught to the students in the large group or small groups, and which could be appropriately learned and reinforced through product menus. The novel unit is then designed using formal instructional large-group lessons, smaller informal group lessons, and specific menu days where the students will use the menu independently to reinforce the prior knowledge they have already learned. In order for this option to be effective, the teacher must feel very comfortable with the students' prior knowledge level, their reading levels, and their readiness to work independently.

Flipped Classroom Activities

> *"Menus make all the difference in the success of my flipped classroom."*
>
> —Middle school teacher

The idea of choice fits hand-in-hand with the philosophy of flipped instruction or the flipped classroom model. When using flipped instruction, the goal is that the students acquire basic information needed through outside sources such as videos, PowerPoint presentations, or other sources their teacher has selected for them. In the case of a novel study, rather than reading the novel aloud round-robin format, students will be responsible for reading sections of the book independently, outside of the classroom. This may mean the students are sitting down at home and reading to themselves, watching a video of the story being read by the author, or listening to an audio recording of the necessary pages. No matter how they have "read" the pages, when the students return to class, their time is spent on quality activities and products based on their reading outside of the classroom. Because the methods students use to read the material are varied, logically, it would work best if the activities within the classroom are varied as well. Using a menu of options to offer and manage the activities and processing experiences will allow all of the different ability levels within the classroom to feel successful.

Using Leveled Menus With Your Students

> *"His is different than mine."*
>
> —Student in a differentiated classroom

This book contains tiered or leveled menus for each of the included novels, stories, or poems. Although the reading material is the same, each of the three menus may have different values assigned to the same task, slightly different wording for similar tasks, the same product options in a different formatted menu, or even tasks that are only available on certain menus. All of these small modifications make certain menus more appropriate for different students based on their readiness, interest, and ability levels.

As we all know, secondary students tend to compare answers, work, and ideas, and their choices on menus are not any different. Although students may notice the slight differences mentioned above, it may not be an issue when students are working in ability groups, as students are comfortable with having different options based on their grouping. It may also not be an issue when the menus are presented matter-of-factly, stating that everyone is getting a menu that was specifically selected for him or her. Students should rest assured that target numbers (goal of 100 is a 100%) are equal for all of the menus provided and the activities often perceived as the "best" or "most fun" by students are found on all of the versions of the menu. Students should also know that most of the menus have a free choice proposal option so if they really want to do one of the activities found on another menu in the classroom, they are welcome to submit that activity on a free choice proposal form. By presenting tiered menus with confidence and an air for uniquely selecting each menu for its recipient, students are usually willing to proceed with the menu they have received.

"That's not fair . . ."

—Said by at least one student every second
in classrooms across the nation

That being said, you may still have a few students who say, in that dreaded middle-school nasal and accusatory tone, "That's still not fair!" When I first starting using leveled menus with my eighth graders, I heard a few comments like this. They quickly dissipated with my standard and practiced responses. Of course, the first response (which they do not always appreciate) is that fair is not equal. I know students do not like to hear this response, as it is hard to argue against this, because it is patently true. Secondly, I remind students that everyone has different strengths and the menus are distributed based on everyone's strengths. Again, they know this; they just do not like to acknowledge it. Lastly, if the students are being especially surly, I sometimes have to play the "parent card," meaning, I am the teacher and I have the right to do what I feel is best for each student. This last option is nonnegotiable and although students may not like it, they understand the tone and sentiment, as they have usually experienced it before at home.

The bottom line when it comes to using tiered menus is that students will respond to the use of seemingly different menus within one classroom based on how the teacher presents or reacts to it. In the past, when I have used different formats, I address the format or obvious differences in a matter-of-fact manner, such as, "I have spiced things up with this menu and have three different ones that I will pass out. You may receive one that is different than your neighbor's but whichever one you receive is going to be lots of fun for you!" Other times, when the menus are very similar in their format and graphics, I just distribute them and address concerns when they are brought up. For the most part, students are more likely to simply go with what they have been given when any differences in menus are presented confidently without being open to debate or complaint.

CHAPTER 3

Guidelines for Products

> "... I got to do a play! In math!"
>
> —Seventh-grade student

This chapter outlines the different types of products used in the featured menus, as well as the guidelines and expectations for each. It is very important that students understand the expectations of a completed product before they choose to work on it. By discussing these expectations before students begin and having the information readily available at the time of product selection, you will limit the frustration on everyone's part.

$1 Contract

> *"I really appreciate the $1 form. It kept me from having to run to [craft store] and spend $60 on felt and glitter and all of the other things we normally have to buy for projects."*
>
> —Parent of one of my students when asked
> for feedback on a recent menu

Consideration should be given to the cost of creating the products included on any menu. The resources available to students vary within a classroom, and students should not be graded on the amount of materials they can purchase to make a product look better. These menus are designed to equalize the resources students have available. The materials for most products are available for less than a dollar and can often be found in a teacher's classroom as part of the classroom supplies. If a product requires materials from the student, a $1 contract is noted as part of the product's guidelines. This is a very important in the explanation of the product. First of all, by limiting the amount of money a child can spend, it creates an equal amount of resources for all students. Second, it actually encourages a more creative product; when students are limited by the amount of materials they can readily purchase, they often have to use materials from home in new and unique ways. Figure 3.1 is a sample of the contract that has been used many times in my classroom with various products.

$1 Contract

I did not spend more than $1.00 on my _____.

_____   _____
               Student Signature   Date

My child, _____, did not spend more than $1.00 on the product he or she created.

_____   _____
               Parent Signature   Date

Figure 3.1. $1 contract.

The Products

Table 3.1 contains a list of the products used in this book. These products were chosen for their flexibility in addressing various learning styles, as well as being popular products most students have experienced; teachers may already be using these in their classroom, which makes the product easy for the students to understand. The products have been sorted by learning style—visual, kinesthetic, or auditory. Each menu has been designed to include products from all of the learning styles. Some of the products may fit into more than one area depending on how they are presented or implemented (and some of the best products cross over between styles), but you will find them listed by their most common application. The specific guidelines for all of the products are presented in an easy-to-read card format that can be reproduced for students. This format is convenient for students to have in front of them when they work on their products.

Product Frustrations

One of the biggest frustrations that accompanies the use of various products on menus is the barrage of questions about the products themselves. Students can become so wrapped up in the products and the criteria for creating them that they do not focus on the content being presented. This is especially true when menus are first introduced to the class. Students can spend an exorbitant amount of time asking the teacher about the products mentioned on the menu. When this happens, what should have been a 10–15 minute menu introduction turns into 45–50 minutes of discussion about product expectations. Most teachers cannot afford to spend even a little time discussing the attributes of a PowerPoint presentation when there is content to be discussed.

Another frustration often comes when showing students product examples. In order to facilitate the introduction of the menu products, teachers may consider showing their students examples of the product(s) from the previous year. Although this can be helpful, it can also lead to additional frustration on the part of both the teacher and the student. Some students may not feel they can produce a product as nice, big, special, or (you fill in the blank) as the example, or when shown an example, take that to mean the teacher would like something exactly like the one they are shown. To avoid this situation, I would propose that, if using examples, the example students are shown be a "blank" example that demonstrates how to create the shell of the product. If an example of a windowpane is needed, for example, then students might be shown a blank piece of paper that is divided into six panes. The students can then take the "skeleton" of the

Table 3.1
Products

Visual	Kinesthetic	Auditory
Acrostic	Board Game	Children's Book
Advertisement	Bulletin Board Display	Commercial/Infomercial
Book Cover	Class Game	Game Show
Brochure/Pamphlet	Commercial/Infomercial	Interview
Bulletin Board Display	Concentration Cards	News Report
Cartoon/Comic Strip	Cross-Cut Diagram/Model	Oral Presentation of Created
Children's Book	Diorama	Product
Class Lesson—Written Only	Experiment	Play/Skit
Collage	Flipbook	PowerPoint—Speaker
Collection	Folded Quiz Book	Puppet
Cross-Cut Diagram/Model	Mobile	Song/Rap
Crossword Puzzle	Model	Speech
Data Table	Mural	Student-Taught Lesson
Drawing	Museum Exhibit	Video
Essay	Play/Skit	You Be the Person
Folded Quiz Book	Product Cube	Presentation
Graph	Puppet	
Graphic Novel	Quiz Board	
Greeting Card	Sculpture	
Instruction Card	Student-Taught Lesson	
Journal/Diary	Three-Dimensional Timeline	
Letter	Trophy	
Map	Video	
Mind Map		
Newspaper Article		
Paragraph		
Pie Graph		
Poster		
PowerPoint—Stand Alone		
Questionnaire		
Quiz		
Recipe Card		
Scrapbook		
Story		
Summary		
Survey		
Three Facts and a Fib		
Trading Cards		
Venn Diagram		
Video		
WebQuest		
Windowpane		
Worksheet		

product and make it their own as they create their own version of the window-pane using their information.

Product Guidelines

> *"Wow. You know how great these are . . . how much time they will save?"*
>
> —A group of teachers, when presented with a page
> of products guidelines for their classroom

Most frustrations associated with products can be addressed proactively through the use of standardized, predetermined product guidelines that are shared with students prior to their selecting and subsequently creating any products. These product guidelines are designed in a specific yet generic way, such that anytime throughout the school year that the students select a product, its guidelines will apply. A beneficial side effect of using set guidelines for a product is the security it creates. Students are often reticent to try something new, as it requires taking a risk on their part. Traditionally, when students select products, they ask questions about creating it; hope they remember and understood all of the details and turn it in. It can be quite a surprise when they receive the product back and realize that it was not complete, or did not meet the teacher's expectations. As you can imagine, students may not want to take the risk on something new the next time; they would prefer to do what they know and be successful. Through the use of product guidelines, students can begin to feel secure in their choice of product before they start working on the product itself. If they are not feeling secure, they tend to stay within their comfort zone.

The product guidelines for all of the menu products, as well as some potential free-choice options, are included in an easy-to-read card format (see Figure 3.2). (The guidelines for some products, such as summaries, are omitted because teachers often have different criteria for these products.) Once the products and/or menus have been selected, there are many options available to share this information.

Sharing Product Guidelines With Students

There really is no one "right way" to share the product guideline information with your students. It all depends on their abilities and needs. Some teachers choose to duplicate and distribute all of the product guideline pages to students at the beginning of the year so each child has his own copy in front of him while he works on his products. As another option, a few classroom sets can be created by gluing each product guideline onto separate index cards, hole punching the corner of each card, and placing them on a metal ring. These ring sets can be placed in a central location, or at a center where students can borrow and return them as they work on their products. Using a ring also allows for the addition of new products as they are introduced to the whole class or through future menus. Some teachers prefer to introduce product guidelines as students experience them on their menus. In this case, product guidelines from the menu currently assigned can be enlarged, laminated, and posted on a bulletin board for easy access during classroom work time. Some teachers may choose to reproduce each menu's specific product guidelines on the back of the menu. No matter which method a teacher chooses to share the information with the students, he or she will save a lot of time and frustration by having the product guidelines available for student reference (e.g., "Look at your product guidelines, I think that will answer your question.")

Story Map

One of the most commonly used products in a language arts classroom is the story map. The story map is a quick and effective way for a student to dissect a story and show that he or she can analyze the important parts of the story. Story maps are an option for many of the menus provided in this book. Three examples are offered (see Figures 3.3, 3.4, and 3.5); each coded to match the levels found in the tiered menus; however, teachers who have a favorite format that students are accustomed to should feel free to use their own.

Acrostic	Advertisement	Board Game
• Must be at least 8.5" by 11" • Neatly written or typed • Target word written down the left side of the paper • Each descriptive phrase chosen must begin with one of the letters from the target word • Each descriptive phrase chosen must be related to the target word	• Must be at least 8.5" by 11" • A slogan should be included • Color picture of item or service should be included • Include price, if appropriate • Can be created on the computer	• At least four thematic game pieces • At least 20 colored/thematic squares • At least 15 question/activity cards • Include a thematic title on the board • Include a complete set of rules for playing the game • At least the size of an open file folder
Book Cover	**Brochure/Pamphlet**	**Bulletin Board Display**
• Front cover—title, author, image • Front inside flap—paragraph summary of the book • Back inside flap—brief biography of author with at least three details • Back cover—your comments about the book • Spine—title and author	• Must be at least 8.5" by 11" • Must be in three-fold format; front fold has the title and picture • Must have both pictures and written text • Information should be in paragraph form with at least five facts included • Can be created on computer	• Must fit within assigned space on bulletin board or wall • Must include at least five details • Must have a title • Must have at least five different elements (e.g., posters, papers, questions) • Must have at least one interactive element that engages the reader
Cartoon/Comic Strip	**Children's Book**	**Class Game**
• Must be at least 8.5" by 11" • Must have at least six cells • Must have meaningful dialogue • Must include color	• Must have a cover with book's title and student's name as author • Must have at least 10 pages • Each page should have an illustration to accompany the story • Neatly written or typed • Can be created on the computer	• Game should allow all class members to participate • Must have only a few, easy-to-understand rules • Can be a new variation on a current game • Must have multiple questions • Must provide answer key before game is played • Must be approved by teacher before being played

Figure 3.2. Product guidelines.

Class Lesson—Written Only	Collage	Collection
(Note: For a class lesson that is presented, use the student-taught lesson rubric.) • Is original—do not just print or copy an activity as is • States the objectives that will be taught • Includes at least one warm-up question • Presents the information in a clear way • Includes all of the important information • Has a way for students to practice the content • Includes a quiz or method of assessment	• Must be at least 8.5" by 11" • Pictures must be cut neatly from magazines or newspapers (no clip art from the computer or the Internet) • Label items as required in task	• Contains number of items stated in task • All items must fit in the space designated by the teacher • All items must be brought to class in a box or bag • No living things!
Commercial/Infomercial	**Concentration Cards**	**Cross-Cut Diagram/Model**
• Must be 1–2 minutes in length • Script must be turned in before the commercial is presented • Can be presented live to an audience or recorded • Should have props or some form of costume(s) • Can include more than one person	• At least 20 index cards (10 matching sets) must be made • Both pictures and words can be used • Information should be placed on just one side of each card • Include an answer key that shows the matches • All cards must be submitted in a carrying bag	• Must include a scale to show the relationship between the diagram/model and the actual item • Must include details for each layer • If creating a diagram, must also meet the guidelines for a poster • If creating a model, must also meet the guidelines for a model
Crossword Puzzle	**Data Table**	**Diorama**
• At least 20 significant words or phrases should be included • Develop appropriate clues • Include puzzle and answer key • Can be created on the computer	• Table and data have proper units, titles, and descriptions • All data should be recorded neatly and be easy to read • If created by hand, all lines should be straight and neat	• Must be at least 4" by 5" by 8" • Must be self-standing • All interior space must be covered with relevant pictures and information • Name written on the back • Informational/title card attached to diorama • $1 contract signed

Figure 3.2. Continued.

Drawing	Essay	Experiment
• Must be at least 8.5" by 11" • Must show what is requested in the task statement • Must include color • Must be neatly drawn by hand • Must have title • Name written on the back	• Neatly written or typed • Must cover the specific topic in detail • Must be at least three paragraphs • Must include resources or bibliography if appropriate	• Includes a hypothesis or purpose • States specific materials for experiment • Includes detailed procedures and data • Includes a written conclusion in paragraph form • Information neatly written or typed as a report

Flipbook	Folded Quiz Book	Game Show
• Must be at least 8.5" by 11" folded in half • All information or opinions are supported by facts • Created with the correct number of flaps cut into the top • Color is optional • Name written on the back	• Must be at least 8.5" by 11" folded in half • Must have at least 10 questions • Created with the correct number of flaps cut into the top • Questions written or typed neatly on upper flaps • Answers written or typed neatly inside each flap • Color is optional • Name written on the back	• Needs an emcee or host • Must have at least two contestants • Must have at least one regular round and a bonus round • Questions will be content specific • Props can be used, but are not mandatory

Graph	Graphic Novel	Greeting Card
• Must have a title • Axes must be labeled with units • All data must be clearly represented • Can be created on the computer • If created by hand, must use graph paper	• Should use color • Must tell a story • Should be at least 10 pages in length • Can be created on the computer	• Front—colored pictures, words optional • Front inside—personal note related to topic • Back inside—greeting or saying; must meet product criteria • Back outside—logo, publisher, and price for card

Figure 3.2. Continued.

Instruction Card	Interview	Journal/Diary
• Must be no larger than 5" by 8" • Created on heavy paper or index card • Neatly written or typed • Uses color drawings • Provides instructions stated in the task	• Must have at least eight questions about the topic being studied • Person chosen for interview must be an "expert" and qualified to provide answers • Questions and answers must be neatly written or typed	• Neatly written or typed • Should include the appropriate number of entries • Should include a date if appropriate • Should be written in first person
Letter	**Map**	**Mind Map**
• Neatly written or typed • Uses proper letter format • At least three paragraphs in length • Must follow type of letter stated in the menu (e.g., friendly, persuasive, informational)	• Must be at least 8.5" by 11" • Accurate information is included • Includes at least 10 relevant locations • Includes compass rose, legend, scale, and key	• Must be at least 8.5" by 11" • Uses unlined paper • Must have one central idea • Follows the "no more than four" rule—no more than four words coming from any one word • Should be neatly written or developed using a computer
Mobile	**Model**	**Mural**
• Includes at least 10 pieces of related information • Includes color and pictures • At least three layers of hanging information • Hangs in a balanced way	• Must be at least 8" by 8" by 12" • Parts of model must be labeled • Should be in scale if possible • Must include a title card • Name should be permanently written on the model • $1 contract signed	• Must be at least 22" x 54" • Must contain at least five pieces of important information • Must have colored pictures • Words are optional, but a title should be included • Name should be permanently written on the back

Figure 3.2. Continued.

Museum Exhibit	News Report	Newspaper Article
• Should have title for exhibit • Must include at least five "artifacts" • Each artifact must be labeled with a neatly written card • Exhibit must fit within the size assigned • $1 contract required • No expensive or irreplaceable objects in the display	• Must address the who, what, where, when, why, and how of the topic • Script of report must be turned in with project (or before if performance will be live) • Must be either performed live or recorded	• Must be informational in nature • Must follow standard newspaper format • Must include picture with caption that supports article • At least three paragraphs in length • Neatly written or typed
Paragraph	**Picture Dictionary**	**Pie Graph**
• Neatly written or typed • Must have topic sentence, at least three supporting sentences or details, and a concluding sentence • Must use appropriate vocabulary and follow grammar rules	• Includes the vocabulary word • Includes a definition in your own words • Includes a picture or drawing that represents the word • Includes the quote where the word is found in the story	• Must have a title • Must have a label for each area or be color coded with a key • Must include the percentages for each area of the graph • Calculations must be provided if needed to create the pie graph • Should be created neatly by hand or using a computer
Play/Skit	**Poster**	**PowerPoint—Speaker**
• Must be 4–6 minutes in length • Script must be turned in before play is presented • May be presented to an audience or recorded for future showing • Should have props or some form of costume(s) • Can include more than one person	• Should be the size of a standard poster board • Includes at least five pieces of important information • Must have title • Must contain both words and pictures • Name written on the back • Bibliography included as needed	• At least 10 informational slides and one title slide with student's name • No more than two words per page • Slides must have color and no more than one graphic per page • Animations are optional but should not distract from information being presented • Presentation should be timed and flow with the speech being given

Figure 3.2. Continued.

PowerPoint—Stand Alone	Product Cube	Puppet
• At least 10 informational slides and one title slide with student's name • No more than 10 words per page • Slides must have color and no more than one graphic per page • Animations are optional but should not distract from information being presented	• All six sides of the cube must be filled with information • Neatly written or typed • Name must be printed neatly on the bottom of one of the sides • Should be submitted flat for grading	• Puppet should be handmade and must have a moveable mouth • A list of supplies used to make the puppet must be turned in with the puppet • $1 contract signed • If used in a puppet show, must also meet the criteria for a play
Questionnaire	**Quiz**	**Quiz Board**
• Neatly written or typed • Include at least 10 questions with possible answers, and at least one answer that requires a written response • Questions must be helpful to gathering information on the topic being studied	• Must be at least a half sheet of paper long • Neatly written or typed • Must cover the specific topic in detail • Must include at least five questions including a short answer question • Must have at least one graphic • An answer key must be turned in with the quiz	• Must have at least five questions • Must have at least five answers • Should use a system with lights • Should be no larger than a poster board • Holiday lights can be used • $1 contract signed
Recipe Card	**Scrapbook**	**Sculpture**
• Must be written neatly or typed on a piece of paper or an index card • Must have a list of ingredients with measurement for each • Must have numbered steps that explain how to make the recipe	• Cover of scrapbook must have a meaningful title and student's name • Must have at least five themed pages • Each page will have at least one meaningful picture • All photos must have captions	• Must be no larger than 24" tall • Must use recycled materials • Must be created from the number of items given in the task • If appropriate, $1 contract must be submitted with sculpture • Creator's name should be permanently written on the base or bottom

Figure 3.2. Continued.

Song/Rap	Speech	Story
• Words must make sense • Can be presented to an audience or taped • Written words must be turned in before performance or with taped song • Should be at least 2 minutes in length	• Must be at least 2 minutes in length • Should not be read from written paper • Note cards can be used • Written speech must be turned in before speech is presented • Voice must be clear, loud, and easy to understand	• Must have all of the elements of a well-written story (setting, characters, conflict, rising action, and resolution) • Must be appropriate length to allow for story elements • Neatly written or typed
Survey	**Tell a Story**	**Three-Dimensional Timeline**
• Must have at least five questions related to the topic • Must include at least one adult respondent who is not your teacher • The respondent must sign the survey • Information gathered and conclusions drawn from the survey should be written or presented graphically	• Has all of the elements of a well-written story • Should be long enough for the story to make sense • Told to teacher or prerecoded	• Must be no bigger than standard-size poster board • Must be divided into equal time units • Must contain at least 10 important dates and have at least two sentences explaining why each date is important • Must have a meaningful object securely attached beside each date to represent that date • Must be able to explain how each object represents each date
Three Facts and a Fib	**Trading Cards**	**Trophy**
• Can be written, typed, or created using PowerPoint • Must include exactly four statements: three true statements and one false statement • False statement should not be obvious • Brief paragraph should be included that explains why the fib is false	• Include at least 10 cards • Each card must be at least 3" by 5" • Each should have a colored picture • Includes at least three facts on the subject of the card • Cards must have information on both sides • All cards must be submitted in a carrying bag	• Must be at least 6" tall • Must have a base with the name of the person getting the trophy and the name of the award written neatly or typed on it • Top of trophy must be appropriate and represent the award • Name should be written on the bottom of the award • Must be an originally designed trophy (avoid reusing a trophy from home) • $1 contract signed

Figure 3.2. Continued.

Venn Diagram	Video	WebQuest
• Must be at least 8.5" by 11" • Shapes should be thematic and neatly drawn • Must have a title for entire diagram and a title for each section • Must have at least six items in each section of the diagram • Name written on the back	• Use VHS, DVD, or Flash format or other recording format • Turn in a written plan with project • Students will need to arrange their own way to record the video or allow teacher at least 3 days notice to set up recording • Covers important information about the project • Name written on the video label	• Must quest through at least three high-quality websites • Websites should be linked in the document • Can be submitted in a Word or PowerPoint document • Includes at least three questions for each website • Must address the topic
Windowpane	Worksheet	You Be the Person Presentation
• Must be at least 8.5" by 11" unlined paper • Must include at least six squares • Each square must include both a picture and words that should be neatly written or typed • All pictures should be both creative and meaningful • Name should be written on the bottom right-hand corner of the front of the windowpane	• Must be 8.5" by 11" • Neatly written or typed • Must cover the specific topic or question in detail • Must have at least one graphic • An answer key will be turned in with the worksheet	• Take on the role of the person • Cover at least five important facts about the life of the person • Must be 3–5 minutes in length • Script must be turned in before information is presented • Should be presented to an audience with the ability to answer questions while in character • Must have props or some form of costume

Figure 3.2. Continued.

Story Map

Title and Author

Setting

Main Characters
Write at least three traits for each main character.

Supporting Characters
Write one sentence about why each supporting character is important to the story.

Problem

Major Events in the Story

Solution

Figure 3.3. Story map 1.

Story Map

Title and Author	**Setting**

Main Characters
For each main character, write at least three traits and a quote from the story to support your chosen traits.

Supporting Characters
Write one sentence about why each supporting character is important to the story.

Problem

Figure 3.4. Story map 2.

Story Map

Major Events in the Story

Resolution

Figure 3.4. Continued.

Story Map

<table>
<tr><td>

Title and Author

</td><td>

Setting

</td></tr>
</table>

Main Characters

Write at least three traits for each character and a quote from the story to support each of your chosen traits.

Supporting Characters

Write one sentence about why each is important to the story.

Problem

Figure 3.5. Story map 3.

Story Map

Major Events in Story

Resolution

Figure 3.5. Continued.

CHAPTER 4

Rubrics

I frequently end up with more papers and products to grade than with a unit taught in the traditional way. Luckily, the rubric speeds up the process."

—Eighth-grade teacher when asked about what she liked least about using menus

The most common reason teachers feel uncomfortable with menus is the need for equality in grading. Teachers often feel it is easier to grade identical products created by all of the students, rather than grading a large number of different products, none of which looks like any other. The great equalizer for a multitude of different products is a generic rubric that can cover all of the important qualities of an excellent product.

All-Purpose Rubric

Figure 4.1 is an example of a rubric that has been classroom tested with various menus. This rubric can be used with any point value activity presented in a menu, as there are five criteria and the columns represent full points, half points, or no points. Although Tic-Tac-Toe and Meal menus are not point based, this rubric can be used to grade products from these menus. Teachers simply assign 100 points to each of the products students select and then use the all-purpose rubric to grade each product individually based on a total of 100 points.

There are different ways that this rubric can be shared with students. Some teachers prefer to provide it when a menu is presented to students. This rubric can be reproduced on the back of the menu along with its guidelines. The rubric can also be given to students to keep in their folder with their product guideline cards so they always know the expectations as they complete products throughout the school year. Some teachers prefer to keep a master copy for themselves and post an enlarged copy of the rubric on a bulletin board, or provide one copy for parents during open house so they understand how their children's menu products will be graded.

No matter how the rubric is shared with students, the first time they see this rubric, it should be explained in detail, especially the last column titled "Self." It is very important that students self-evaluate their products. This column can provide a unique perspective of the project as it is being graded. *Note*: This rubric was designed to be specific enough that students will know the criteria the teacher is seeking, but general enough that they can still be as creative as they like in the creation of their product.

Student-Taught Lessons and Student Presentation Rubrics

Although the all-purpose rubric can be used for all activities, there are two occasions that seem to warrant a special rubric: student-taught lessons and student presentations. These are unique situations, with many details that must be considered to create a quality product.

Teachers often would like to allow students to teach their fellow classmates, but are concerned about quality lessons and may not be comfortable with the grading aspect of the assignment; rarely do students understand all of the components that go into designing an effective lesson. This student-taught lesson rubric helps focus the student on the important aspects of a well-designed lesson, and allows teachers to make the evaluation process a little more subjective. The student-taught lesson rubric (see Figure 4.2) included for these menus is appropriate for all levels.

Student presentations can be difficult to evaluate. The first consideration with these types of presentations is that of objectivity. The objectivity can be addressed through a very specific presentation rubric that reinforces the expec-

Name: _____

All-Purpose Rubric

Criteria	Excellent (Full Credit)	Good (Half Credit)	Poor (No Credit)	Self
Content Is the content of the product well chosen?	Content chosen represents the best choice for the product. Information or graphics are well chosen and related to content.	Information or graphics are related to content, but are not the best choice for the product.	Information or graphics presented do not appear to be related to the topic or task.	
Completeness Is everything included in the product?	All information needed is included. Product meets the product criteria and the criteria of the task as stated.	Some important information is missing. Product meets the product criteria and the criteria of the task as stated.	Most important information is missing. The product does not meet the task or does not meet the product criteria.	
Creativity Is the product original?	Presentation of information is from a new perspective. Graphics are original. Product includes elements of fun and interest.	Presentation of information is from a new perspective. Graphics are not original. Product has elements of fun and interest.	There is no evidence of new thoughts or perspectives in the product.	
Correctness Is all of the information included correct?	All information presented in the product is correct and accurate.	Not applicable.	Any portion of the information presented in the product is incorrect.	
Communication Is the information in the product well communicated?	All information is neat and easy to read. Product is in appropriate format and shows significant effort. Oral presentations are easy to understand and presented with fluency.	Most of the product is neat and easy to read. Product is in appropriate format and shows significant effort. Oral presentations are easy to understand, with some fluency.	The product is not neat and easy to read or the product is not in the appropriate format. It does not show significant effort. Oral presentation was not fluent or easy to understand.	
			Total Grade:	

Figure 4.1. All-purpose product rubric.

Name: _____

Student-Taught Lesson Grading Rubric

Parts of Lesson	Excellent	Good	Fair	Poor	Self
Prepared and Ready: All materials and lesson ready at start of class period, from warm-up to conclusion of lesson.	**10** Everything is ready to present.	**6** Lesson is present, but small amount of scrambling.	**3** Lesson is present, but major scrambling.	**0** No lesson ready or missing major components.	
Understanding: Presenter understands the material well. Students understand information presented.	**20** All information is correct and in correct format.	**12** Presenter understands; 25% of students do not.	**4** Presenter understands; 50% of students do not.	**0** Presenter is confused.	
Completion: Includes all significant information from section or topic.	**15** Includes all important information.	**10** Includes most important information.	**2** Includes less than 50% of the important information.	**0** Information is not related.	
Practice: Includes some way for students to practice or access the information.	**20** Practice present, well chosen.	**10** Practice present, can be applied effectively.	**5** Practice present, not related or best choice.	**0** No practice or students are confused.	
Interest/Fun: Most of the class is involved, interested, and participating.	**15** Everyone interested and participating.	**10** 75% actively participating.	**5** Less than 50% actively participating.	**0** Everyone off task.	
Creativity: Information presented in imaginative way.	**20** Wow, creative! I never would have thought of that!	**12** Good ideas!	**5** Some good pieces but general instruction.	**0** No creativity; all lecture/ notes/ worksheet.	
				Total Grade:	

Your Topic/Objective:

Comments:

Don't Forget:
All copy requests and material requests must be made at least 24 hours in advance.

_____

Figure 4.2. Student-taught lesson grading rubric.

tations for the speaker. The rubric will need to be discussed and various criteria demonstrated before the students begin preparing their presentations. The second consideration is that of the audience and its interest in the presentation. How frustrating is it to have to grade 30 presentations when the audience is not paying attention, off task, or tuning out? This can be solved by allowing your audience to be directly involved in the presentation by presenting them with a rubric that can be used to provide feedback to their classmates. If all of the students have been instructed on the student presentation rubric (see Figure 4.3) when they receive their feedback rubric, then they will be quite comfortable with the criteria. Students are asked to rank their classmates on a scale of 1–10 in the areas of content, flow, and the prop they chose to enhance their presentation (see Figure 4.4). Students are also asked to state two things the presenter did well. Although most students understand this should be a positive experience for the presenter, it may need to be reinforced that certain types of feedback are not necessary; for example, if the presenter dropped her prop and had to pick it up, the presenter knows this and it probably does not need to be noted again. The feedback should be positive and specific as well. A comment of "Great!" is not what should be recorded; instead, something specific such as, "You spoke loudly and clearly" or "You had great drawings!" should be written on the form. These types of comments really make the students take note and feel great about their presentations. The teacher should not be surprised to note that the students often look through all of their classmates' feedback and comments before ever consulting the rubric the teacher completed. Once students have completed a feedback form for a presenter, the forms can then be gathered at the end of each presentation, stapled together, and given to the presenter at the end of the class.

Name: _____

Student Presentation Rubric

Criteria	Excellent	Good	Fair	Poor	Self
Content Complete Did the presentation include everything it should?	**30** Presentation included all important information about topic being presented.	**20** Presentation covered most of the important information, but one key idea was missing.	**10** Presentation covered some of the important information, but more than one key idea was missing.	**0** Presentation covered information, but the information was trivial or fluff.	
Content Correct Was the information presented accurate?	**30** All information presented was accurate.	**20** All information presented was correct, with a few unintentional errors that were quickly corrected.	Not applicable.	**0** Any information presented was not correct.	
Prop Did the speaker have at least one prop that was directly related to the presentation?	**20** Presenter had a prop and it complemented the presentation.	**12** Presenter had a prop, but it was not the best choice.	**4** Presenter had a prop, but there was no clear reason for it.	**0** Presenter had no prop.	
Content Consistent Did the speaker stay on topic?	**10** Presenter stayed on topic 100% of the time.	**7** Presenter stayed on topic 90%–99% of the time.	**4** Presenter stayed on topic 80%–89% of the time.	**0** It was hard to tell what the topic was.	
Flow Was the speaker familiar and comfortable with the material so that it flowed well?	**10** Presentation flowed well. Speaker did not stumble over words.	**7** Presenter had some flow problems, but they did not distract from information.	**4** Some flow problems interrupted the presentation, and presenter seemed flustered.	**0** Constant flow problems occurred, and information was not presented so that it could be understood.	
				Total Grade:	

Figure 4.3. Student presentation rubric.

Topic: _____   **Student's Name:** _____

On a scale of 1–10, rate the following areas:

Content (How in depth was the information? How well did the speaker know the information? Was the information correct? Could the speaker answer questions?)		Give one short reason why you gave this number.
Flow (Did the presentation flow smoothly? Did the speaker appear confident and ready to speak?)		Give one short reason why you gave this number.
Prop (Did the speaker explain his or her prop? Did this choice seem logical? Was it the best choice?)		Give one short reason why you gave this number.

Comments: Below, write two things that you think the presenter did well:

1.

2.

- -

Topic: _____   **Student's Name:** _____

On a scale of 1–10, rate the following areas:

Content (How in depth was the information? How well did the speaker know the information? Was the information correct? Could the speaker answer questions?)		Give one short reason why you gave this number.
Flow (Did the presentation flow smoothly? Did the speaker appear confident and ready to speak?)		Give one short reason why you gave this number.
Prop (Did the speaker explain his or her prop? Did this choice seem logical? Was it the best choice?)		Give one short reason why you gave this number.

Comments: Below, write two things that you think the presenter did well:

1.

2.

Figure 4.4. Student feedback form.

51

The Menus

The stories, novels, and poems that have been selected for inclusion in this book are found on the list of text exemplars in Appendix B of the Common Core State Standards for English Language Arts, which can be accessed at http://www.corestandards.org/assets/Appendix_B.pdf.

How to Use the Menu Pages

Each menu in this section has:

- an introduction page for the teacher;
- a highly modified menu, indicated by a triangle (▲) in the upper right hand corner;
- a moderately modified menu, indicated by a circle (●) in the upper right hand corner
- an unmodified, advanced menu, indicated by a square (■) in the upper right hand corner and,
- any specific activities mentioned on the menus.

Introduction Pages

The introduction pages are meant to provide an overview of each menu. They are divided into various areas.

1. *Title and Menu Type.* The top of each introductory page will note the title of the story, novel, or poem as well as the menu type(s) used. Each novel included has three menus, a highly modified menu (▲), a slightly modified/on-level menu (●), and an advanced menu (■). When possible, all three menus are in the same format, however, sometimes in order to modify for special needs students, the lowest level menu may have a different format to control the amount of choice a student faces at one time. The Poetry Shape menus cover all three levels within one menu.

2. *Brief Synopsis.* Under the title of the menu, a brief synopsis of the text has been included for teacher reference.

3. *Objectives Covered Through the Menu and Activities.* This area will list all of the objectives that the menu can address. Menus are arranged in such a way that if students complete the guidelines set forth in the menu's instructions, all of these objectives will be covered. Some objectives may be designated with a shape at the end, which indicates that the specific objective is only addressed on its corresponding menu.

4. *Materials Needed by Students for Completion.* The introduction page includes a list of materials that may be needed by students as they complete either menu. Any materials listed that are used in only **one** of the three menus are designated with that menu's corresponding shape code. Students do have the choice in the menu items they would like to complete, so it is possible that the teacher will not need all of these materials for every student. In addition to any materials listed for specific menus, it is expected that the teacher will provide, or students will have access to, the following materials for each menu:
   a. lined paper;
   b. blank 8 1/2" by 11" white paper;
   c. glue; and
   d. crayons, colored pencils, or markers.

5. *Special Notes on the Modifications of These Menus.* Some menu formats have special management issues or considerations when it comes to modifying for different ability levels. This section will review additional options available for modifying each menu.

6. *Special Notes on the Use of This Menu.* Some menus allow students to present demonstrations, experiments, songs, or PowerPoint presentations to their classmates. This section will provide any special tips on managing

products that may require more time, supplies, or space. This section will also share any tips to consider for a specific activity.

7. *Time Frame.* Each menu has its own ideal time frame based on its structure, but all work best with at least a one-week time frame. Menus that assess more objectives are better suited to more than 2 weeks. This section will give you an overview about the best time frame for completing the entire menu, as well as options for shorter time periods. If teachers do not have time to devote to an entire menu, they certainly can choose the 1–2-day option for any menu topic students are currently studying.

8. *Suggested Forms.* This is a list of the rubrics, templates, or reproducibles that should be available for students as the menus are introduced and completed. If a menu has a free-choice option, the appropriate proposal form also will be listed here.

CHAPTER 5

Novels, Short Stories, and Drama

Little Women

List Menu

This is a story of the four unique March sisters, Meg, Jo, Beth and Amy. *Little Women* follows the March family as the girls move from childhood into adulthood. It shares their life lessons, disappointments, and adventures.

Reading Objectives Covered Through These Menus and These Activities

- Students will represent textual evidence and use it to prove conclusions.
- Students will make and explain inferences made from the story.
- Students will make predictions based on what is read.
- Students will show comprehension by summarizing a story.
- Students will represent textual evidence by using story maps.
- Students will compare different forms of a written work (written versus performed).
- Students will analyze characters, their relationships, and their importance in the story.
- Students will recognize and analyze story plot and problem resolution.

Writing Objectives Covered Through These Menus and These Activities

- Students will write to express their feelings, inform, explain, describe, narrate, entertain, persuade, and reflect.
- Students will support their responses with textual evidence.
- Students will exhibit voice in their writing.

Materials Needed by Students for Completion

- *Little Women* by Louisa May Alcott
- Poster board or large white paper
- Materials for board games (folders, colored cards, etc.)
- Microsoft PowerPoint or other slideshow software ■
- Scrapbooking materials ● ■
- Blank index cards (for concentration cards)
- Story map ▲ ●
- DVD or VHS recorder (for news reports)

Special Notes on the Modifications of These Menus

- Because a List menu is a point-based menu, it is easy to provide additional modifications by simply changing the point goal for those students who need it. The bottom of the menu has a short contract that can be used to record any changes. The two-page format of the triangle and circle menu also allow for additional modification by mixing and matching the pages. The front of each of these two-page menus has the lower and middle-level activities, while the second page has the higher level activities and contract. Additional modifications can be made by using the first page from the circle menu with the second page from the triangle menu. This will allow students a little more flexibility when approaching the higher level activities.

Special Notes on the Use of These Menus

- These menus give students the opportunity to create a news report. Although students enjoy producing their own videos, there often are difficulties obtaining the equipment and scheduling the use of a video recorder. This activity can be modified by allowing students to act out the product (like a play) or, if students have the technology, allowing them to produce a webcam version of their presentation.
- The circle menu ● allows students to create a bulletin board display. Some classrooms may only have one bulletin board, so the teacher can divide the board into sections, or additional classroom wall or hall space can be sectioned off for the creation of these displays. Students can plan their display based on the amount of space they are assigned.

Time Frame

- 1–2 weeks—Students are given a menu as the unit is started, and the guidelines and point expectations are discussed. Students usually will need to earn 100 points for 100%, although there is an opportunity for extra credit if the teacher would like to use another target number. Because this menu covers one topic in depth, the teacher will go over all of the options for the topic being covered and have students place check marks in the boxes next to the activities they are most interested in completing. Teachers will need to set aside a few moments to sign the agreement at the bottom of the page with each student. As instruction continues, activities are completed by students and submitted to the teacher for grading.
- 1–2 days—The teacher chooses an activity from the menus to use with the entire class.

Suggested Forms

- All-purpose rubric
- Student presentation rubric
- Proposal form for point-based products

Name: _____ ▲

Little Women: Side 1

Guidelines:

1. You may complete as many of the activities listed within the time period.
2. You may choose any combination of activities.
3. Your goal is 100 points. You may earn up to _____ points extra credit.
4. You may be as creative as you like within the guidelines listed below.
5. You must show your plan to your teacher by _____.
6. Activities may be turned in at any time during the working time period. They will be graded and recorded on this sheet as you continue to work, so keep it safe!

Plan to Do	Activity to Complete (Side 1: 10–25 points)	Point Value	Date Completed	Points Earned
	Make an acrostic for the name of one of the characters in *Little Women*.	10		
	Survey your classmates about which character they like best. Make a poster to share your findings.	15		
	Complete a story map for *Little Women*.	15		
	List at least five other titles that could have been used for *Little Women*.	15		
	Create a picture dictionary for at least 10 "new to you" words from the novel.	15		
	Make a set of concentration cards in which users match character names with a drawing of the character.	15		
	Design a quiz that could be used to test your classmates on their knowledge of the characters in *Little Women*.	20		
	Design an advertisement that could be used to encourage others to read *Little Women*.	25		
	Design a timeline that shows the important events in the story.	25		
	Retell your favorite part of the story for your classmates.	25		
	Total number of points you are planning to earn from Side 1.		**Total points earned from Side 1:**	

Little Women: Side 2

Guidelines:

1. You may complete as many of the activities listed within the time period.
2. You may choose any combination of activities.
3. Your goal is 100 points. You may earn up to _____ points extra credit.
4. You may be as creative as you like within the guidelines listed below.
5. You must show your plan to your teacher by _____.
6. Activities may be turned in at any time during the working time period. They will be graded and recorded on this sheet as you continue to work, so keep it safe!

Plan to Do	Activity to Complete (Side 2: 30–40 points)	Point Value	Date Completed	Points Earned
	Come to school as one of the characters from *Little Women* and discuss your best adventure.	30		
	Make a board game about the adventures the girls experience during the story.	30		
	Mr. March served in the Civil War. Perform a news report that shares information about the Civil War.	30		
	Keep a diary or journal for one of the March sisters. It should have at least five entries to reflect the important events in their lives.	35		
	Which March sister is most like you? Write an essay explaining your decision.	35		
	Design a graphic novel version of *Little Women*.	40		
	A few movies have been made from *Little Women*. Watch one of these movies and give a speech explaining whether you liked the movie or the book better.	40		
	Free choice: Submit your free choice proposal form for a product of your choice.			
	Total number of points you are planning to earn from Side 1.	**Total points earned from Side 1:**		
	Total number of points you are planning to earn from Side 2.	**Total points earned from Side 2:**		
		Grand Total (/100)		

I am planning to complete _____ activities that could earn up to a total of _____ points.

Teacher's initials _____ Student's signature _____

© Prufrock Press Inc. • *Literature for Every Learner* • Grades 6–8
Permission is granted to photocopy or reproduce this page for single classroom use only.

Name: _____   ●

Little Women: Side 1

Guidelines:

1. You may complete as many of the activities listed within the time period.
2. You may choose any combination of activities.
3. Your goal is 100 points. You may earn up to _____ points extra credit.
4. You may be as creative as you like within the guidelines listed below.
5. You must show your plan to your teacher by _____.
6. Activities may be turned in at any time during the working time period. They will be graded and recorded on this sheet as you continue to work, so keep it safe!

Plan to Do	Activity to Complete (Side 1: 10–20 points)	Point Value	Date Completed	Points Earned
	Some critics believe *Little Women* should have a different title. Make a poster to share at least five alternate titles for *Little Women*. Include why you believe each new title is appropriate.	10		
	Complete a story map for *Little Women*.	15		
	Create a picture dictionary for at least 20 "new to you" words from the novel.	15		
	Design a folded quiz book to quiz others on the events that take place in *Little Women*.	15		
	Design a quiz that could be used to test your classmates on their knowledge of the characters in *Little Women*.	15		
	Make a set of concentration cards that has users matching characters with their description based on quotes from the book.	15		
	Make an acrostic for one of the characters in *Little Women*. Use both the first and last name for the character.	15		
	Design a three-dimensional timeline for the important events in the story.	20		
	Design an advertisement that could be used to encourage others to read *Little Women*.	20		
	Turn your favorite part of the story into a play or skit and perform it for the class.	20		
	Total number of points you are planning to earn from Side 1.	**Total points earned from Side 1:**		

Name: _____

Little Women: Side 2

Guidelines:

1. You may complete as many of the activities listed within the time period.
2. You may choose any combination of activities.
3. Your goal is 100 points. You may earn up to _____ points extra credit.
4. You may be as creative as you like within the guidelines listed below.
5. You must show your plan to your teacher by _____.
6. Activities may be turned in at any time during the working time period. They will be graded and recorded on this sheet as you continue to work, so keep it safe!

Plan to Do	Activity to Complete (Side 2: 25–30 points)	Point Value	Date Completed	Points Earned
	Design a bulletin board display that shares information about the historical events that took place during this story.	25		
	Come to school as one of the characters from *Little Women* and discuss your impressions of your sisters.	25		
	Make a board game about the adventures the girls experience during the story.	25		
	Perform a news report about the Civil War. Be sure and interview a chaplain named Mr. March in your report.	25		
	Keep a diary or journal for one of the March sisters. It should have at least 10 entries to reflect the important events found in the story from their perspective.	30		
	A few movies have been made from *Little Women*. After you have finished the novel, watch one of these movies and give a speech comparing to the two works.	30		
	Which March sister is most like you? Write an essay explaining you decision. Be sure and include textual evidence from the book to support your opinion.	30		
	Write a graphic novel version of *Little Women*.	30		
	Free choice: Submit your free choice proposal form for a product of your choice.			
	Total number of points you are planning to earn from Side 1.	**Total points earned from Side 1:**		
	Total number of points you are planning to earn from Side 2.	**Total points earned from Side 2:**		
		Grand Total (/100)		

I am planning to complete _____ activities that could earn up to a total of _____ points.

Teacher's initials _____ Student's signature _____

Name: _____

Little Women

Guidelines:

1. You may complete as many of the activities listed within the time period.
2. You may choose any combination of activities.
3. Your goal is 100 points. You may earn up to _____ points extra credit.
4. You may be as creative as you like within the guidelines listed below.
5. You must show your plan to your teacher by _____.
6. Activities may be turned in at any time during the working time period. They will be graded and recorded on this sheet as you continue to work, so keep it safe!

Plan to Do	Activity to Complete	Point Value	Date Completed	Points Earned
	Make an acrostic for one of the characters in *Little Women*. Use both the first and last name for the character.	10		
	Some critics believe *Little Women* should have a different title. Make a poster to share at least 10 alternate titles for *Little Women*. Include why you believe each of your new titles is appropriate.	10		
	Design a quiz that could be used to test your classmates on their knowledge of the characters in *Little Women*.	10		
	Create a scrapbook of newspaper articles that represent the type of writing Jo enjoyed before Professor Bhaer suggested she write in a different style.	15		
	Design a folded quiz book to quiz others on the events that take place in *Little Women*.	15		
	Make a set of concentration cards that has users matching characters with their descriptions using only quotes from the book.	15		
	Come to school as a character from *Little Women* (not Meg, Jo, Beth, or Amy) and discuss your impressions of each of the girls.	20		
	Design a three-dimensional timeline for the life of one of the sisters. The timeline should focus on events that were significant just for her and how she changes through the novel.	20		
	Make a Part One or a Part Two board game about the adventures the girls experience during this part of the novel.	20		
	Analyze the novel for historical accuracy. Design a PowerPoint presentation that shares information about world events that were taking place during the time period *Little Women* was written. Include how these events were portrayed in the novel.	25		
	A few movie versions have been made of *Little Women*. After finishing the novel, watch one of these movies and write a paper to compare to the two works.	25		
	Perform a news report about the Civil War. Be sure and interview a chaplain named Mr. March in your report.	25		
	Which March sister is most like you? Write an essay explaining your decision. Be sure to include textual evidence from the book to support your opinion.	25		
	Write a graphic novel version of *Little Women*.	25		
	Keep a diary or journal for one of the March sisters. It should have at least 15 entries to reflect important story events from their perspective.	30		
	Free choice: Submit your free choice proposal form for a product of your choice.			
	Total number of points you are planning to earn.	**Total points earned:**		

I am planning to complete _____ activities that could earn up to a total of _____ points.

Teacher's initials _____ Student's signature _____

"The People Could Fly"

20-50-80 Menu

This folktale begins by explaining that although the people of Africa used to have wings and could fly, their wings were shed during their voyage on the slave ships. The readers soon meet two slaves, Sarah, a young mother who carries her child on her back, and Toby, an old man who steps to her aid when she falls. When Sarah's child begins to cry and draws the overseer's whip, Toby decides it is time for those who once had wings to fly again.

Reading Objectives Covered Through These Menus and These Activities

- Students will compare one literary work with another.
- Students will make and explain inferences made from the story.
- Students will make predictions based on what is read.
- Students will show comprehension by summarizing a story.
- Students will analyze characters, their relationships, and their importance in the story.
- Students will recognize and analyze story plot and problem resolution.

Writing Objectives Covered Through These Menus and These Activities

- Students will write to express their feelings, inform, explain, describe, narrate, or entertain.
- Students will exhibit voice in their writing.

Materials Needed by Students for Completion

- "The People Could Fly" by Virginia Hamilton
- *Tar Beach* by Faith Ringgold ■
- Poster board or large white paper
- Internet access (for WebQuests) ■
- DVD or VHS recorder (for videos)
- Recycled materials (for dioramas)
- World map ▲ ●
- Magazines (for collages) ▲ ●

Special Notes on the Modifications of These Menus

- If needed, further modifications can be made to a 20-50-80 menu based on the needs of your students. The easiest modification is altering the point goal from 100; lowering or raising the goal on a menu by 10 (or 20) points is appropriate if additional modification up or down is needed.

Special Notes on the Use of These Menus

- These menus give students the opportunity to create a video. Although students enjoy producing their own videos, there often are difficulties obtaining the equipment and scheduling the use of a video recorder. This activity can be modified by allowing students to act out the product (like a play) or, if students have the technology, allowing them to produce a webcam version of their presentation.
- These menus ask students to use recycled materials to create their diorama. This does not mean only plastic and paper; instead, students should focus on using materials in new ways. It works well if a box is started for "recycled" contributions at the beginning of the school year. That way, students always have access to these types of materials.

Time Frame

- 1–2 weeks—Students are given a menu as the unit is started, and the teacher discusses all of the product options on the menu. As the different options are discussed, students will choose the activities they are most interested in completing so they meet their goal of 100 points. As the lessons progress through the week(s), the teacher and students refer back to the menu options associated with the content being taught.
- 1–2 days—The teacher chooses an activity from the menus to use with the entire class.

Suggested Forms

- All-purpose rubric
- Student presentation rubric
- Proposal form for point-based projects

"The People Could Fly"

Directions: Choose at least two activities from the options below. The activities must total 100 points. Place a checkmark next to each box to show which activities you will complete. All activities must be completed by: _____.

20 points

❏ Use a world map to show the slave routes of the ships. Include where slaves were taken from and where they were transported to in the United States.

❏ Make a drawing that shows what the people may have looked like before they lost their wings.

50 points

❏ Make a collage of words that represent how the people felt while being transported on the slave ships.

❏ Record a video of you telling (not reading) the story of "The People Could Fly" as it might have been told to others around the fire.

❏ Design a diorama to show a scene from the story.

❏ Free choice: Submit a proposal form for a product of your choice.

80 points

❏ Create a song or rap that those without wings may have sung while working to remember the story.

❏ Read another folktale from Virginia Hamilton's book. Make a speech that shares which folktale you liked the best and why.

Name: _____

"The People Could Fly"

Directions: Choose at least two activities from the options below. The activities must total 100 points. Place a checkmark next to each box to show which activities you will complete. All activities must be completed by: _____.

---

20 points

❑ Use a world map to show the slave routes of the ships. Include where slaves were taken from and where they were transported to in different countries.

❑ Make a collage of words that represent how the people felt while being transported on the slave ships.

---

50 points

❑ Record a video of you telling (not reading) the story of "The People Could Fly" as it might have been told to others around the fire at night.

❑ Design a diorama to show the scene in which Toby and the others leave.

❑ Select another folktale from Virginia Hamilton's book. Use a Venn diagram to compare "The People Could Fly" with the folktale you have selected.

❑ Free choice: Submit a proposal form for a product of your choice.

---

80 points

❑ Find a folktale that a population other than African slaves may have used to give hope to those who heard it. Turn the folktale into a children's book with illustrations.

❑ Create a song or rap that those without wings may have sung while working to remember the story.

"The People Could Fly"

Directions: Choose at least two activities from the options below. The activities must total 100 points. Place a checkmark next to each box to show which activities you will complete. All activities must be completed by: _____.

20 points

❑ Record a video of you telling (not reading) the story of "The People Could Fly" as it might have been told to others around the fire at night.

❑ Design a diorama to show the scene in which Toby and the others leave.

50 points

❑ Create a song or rap that those without wings may have sung while working to remember the story.

❑ Write an essay that shares the reasons why this folktale may have been so meaningful to those who heard it.

❑ Read the book *Tar Beach*. Use a Venn diagram to compare this story with "The People Could Fly."

❑ Free choice: Submit a proposal form for a product of your choice.

80 points

❑ Create a WebQuest that shares information on the historical events described in "The People Could Fly," as well as how slavery was ended.

❑ Find a folktale that a population other than African slaves may have used to give hope to those who heard it. Turn this folktale into a children's book with illustrations in the style of those used in "The People Could Fly."

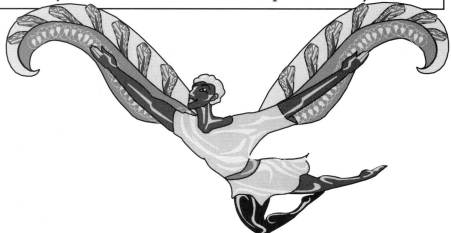

The Dark Is Rising

List Menu

The night before his 11th birthday, Will Stanton, a seventh son of a seventh son, finds his world has suddenly changed. Early on his birthday morning, Will awakes to find himself centuries back in time and discovers that he is actually the last of the "Old Ones," a mystical group whose mission has always been to keep the forces of the Dark under control. Will has been born with a great gift of power, and he must now undertake the heroic quest to find and to join together the six Signs of the Light—for "the Dark is rising."

Reading Objectives Covered Through These Menus and These Activities

- Students will represent textual evidence and use it to prove conclusions.
- Students will make and explain inferences made from the story.
- Students will make predictions based on what is read.
- Students will show comprehension by summarizing a story.
- Students will represent textual evidence by using story maps.
- Students will compare different forms of a written work (written versus performed.)
- Students will analyze characters, their relationships, and their importance in the story.
- Students will recognize and analyze story plot and problem resolution.

Writing Objectives Covered Through These Menus and These Activities

- Students will write to express their feelings, inform, explain, describe, narrate, entertain, influence, persuade, or reflect.
- Students will support their responses with textual evidence.

Materials Needed by Students for Completion

- Poster board or large white paper
- Story map
- Recycled materials (for dioramas, puppets ▲)
- Magazines (for collages)
- Microsoft PowerPoint or other slideshow software ● ■
- DVD or VHS recorder (for commercials, news reports)
- Materials for board games (folders, colored cards, etc.) ▲ ●
- Blank index cards (for mobiles, trading cards, concentration cards) ▲ ●
- Coat hangers (for mobiles) ▲ ●

- String (for mobiles) ▲ ●
- Socks (for puppets) ▲
- Paper bags (for puppets) ▲

Special Notes on the Modifications of These Menus

- Because a List menu is a point-based menu, it is easy to provide additional modifications by simply changing the point goal for those students who need it. The bottom of the menu has a short contract that can be used to record any changes. The two-page format of the triangle and circle menu also allow for additional modification by mixing and matching the pages. The front of each of these two-page menus has the lower and middle-level activities, while the second page has the higher level activities and contract. Additional modifications can be made by using the first page from the circle menu with the second page from the triangle menu. This will allow students a little more flexibility when approaching the higher level activities.

Special Notes on the Use of These Menus

- These menus give students the opportunity to create a commercial and news report. Although students enjoy producing their own videos, there often are difficulties obtaining the equipment and scheduling the use of a video recorder. This activity can be modified by allowing students to act out the product (like a play) or, if students have the technology, allowing them to produce a webcam version of their presentation.
- The triangle menu ▲ asks students to use recycled materials to create their dioramas and puppets. This does not mean only plastic and paper; instead, students should focus on using materials in new ways. It works well if a box is started for "recycled" contributions at the beginning of the school year. That way, students always have access to these types of materials.
- The circle menu ● allows students to create a bulletin board display. Some classrooms may only have one bulletin board, so the teacher can divide the board into sections, or additional classroom wall or hall space can be sectioned off for the creation of these displays. Students can plan their display based on the amount of space they are assigned.

Time Frame

- 1–2 weeks—Students are given a menu as the unit is started, and the guidelines and point expectations are discussed. Students usually will need to earn 100 points for 100%, although there is an opportunity for extra credit if the teacher would like to use another target number. Because this menu covers one topic in depth, the teacher will go over all of the options for the topic being covered and have students place check marks in the boxes next to the activities they are most interested in completing. Teachers will need to set aside a few moments to sign the agreement at the bottom of the page with each student. As instruction continues, activities are completed by students and submitted to the teacher for grading.

- 1–2 days—The teacher chooses an activity from the menus to use with the entire class.

Suggested Forms

- All-purpose rubric
- Student presentation rubric
- Proposal form for point-based products

Name: _____

The Dark Is Rising: Side 1

Guidelines:

1. You may complete as many of the activities listed within the time period.
2. You may choose any combination of activities.
3. Your goal is 100 points. You may earn up to _____ points extra credit.
4. You may be as creative as you like within the guidelines listed below.
5. You must show your plan to your teacher by _____.
6. Activities may be turned in at any time during the working time period. They will be graded and recorded on this sheet as you continue to work, so keep it safe!

Plan to Do	Activity to Complete (Side 1: 15–30 points)	Point Value	Date Completed	Points Earned
	Complete a story map for *The Dark Is Rising*.	15		
	Make an acrostic for the word *dark* or *light* based on the information in the book.	15		
	Retell the most exciting part of *The Dark Is Rising*.	20		
	Create a set of trading cards for the different people Will encounters on his journey.	25		
	Create a mobile for the characters in the book. Under each character, select words the author uses to tell us whether he or she represents the dark or the light.	25		
	Will lives in a rectory. Build a diorama of his home.	25		
	Design a book cover for *The Dark Is Rising*.	25		
	Make a collage of modern-day items that are examples of the different signs of light. Label each item with its sign.	30		
	This book has a lot of time travel. Create a three-dimensional timeline to show all of the events as they happen in the book.	30		
	Total number of points you are planning to earn from Side 1.		**Total points earned from Side 1:**	

The Dark Is Rising: Side 2

Guidelines:

1. You may complete as many of the activities listed within the time period.
2. You may choose any combination of activities.
3. Your goal is 100 points. You may earn up to _____ points extra credit.
4. You may be as creative as you like within the guidelines listed below.
5. You must show your plan to your teacher by _____.
6. Activities may be turned in at any time during the working time period. They will be graded and recorded on this sheet as you continue to work, so keep it safe!

Plan to Do	Activity to Complete (Side 2: 35–45 points)	Point Value	Date Completed	Points Earned
	Will has been considered a hero. Perform a speech in which he discusses all of his adventures and whether he is a hero or not.	35		
	Make a puppet for one of the dark characters in the story. Use your puppet to try and convince Will your side is better.	35		
	Design a board game about *The Dark Is Rising* in which players answer questions while trying to obtain and join the signs of light together.	40		
	There are other books in *The Dark Is Rising* series. Design a commercial to convince your classmates to read the next book in the series.	40		
	Create a news report that shares the consequences for the world if Will cannot attain his goal.	45		
	This book has also been released as a movie. After reading the book, watch the movie and create a Venn diagram that shares their similarities and differences. Include a paragraph that states which format you enjoyed more and why.	45		
	Free choice: Submit your free choice proposal form for a product of your choice.			
	Total number of points you are planning to earn from Side 1.	**Total points earned from Side 1:**		
	Total number of points you are planning to earn from Side 2.	**Total points earned from Side 2:**		
		Grand Total (/100)		

I am planning to complete _____ activities that could earn up to a total of _____ points.

Teacher's initials _____ Student's signature _____

The Dark Is Rising: Side 1

Guidelines:

1. You may complete as many of the activities listed within the time period.
2. You may choose any combination of activities.
3. Your goal is 100 points. You may earn up to _____ points extra credit.
4. You may be as creative as you like within the guidelines listed below.
5. You must show your plan to your teacher by _____.
6. Activities may be turned in at any time during the working time period. They will be graded and recorded on this sheet as you continue to work, so keep it safe!

Plan to Do	Activity to Complete (Side 1: 15–25 points)	Point Value	Date Completed	Points Earned
	Complete a story map for *The Dark Is Rising*.	15		
	Create a set of trading cards for the different people Will encounters on his journey.	20		
	Create a mobile for the characters in the book. Under each character, select words the author uses to tell us whether he or she represents the dark or the light.	20		
	Will lives in a rectory. Consider the evidence in the story and build a diorama of his home.	20		
	Design a book cover for *The Dark Is Rising*.	25		
	Design an advertisement for the light sign that the Walker has been carrying.	25		
	Make a collage of modern-day items that are examples of the different signs of light. Label each item with its sign.	25		
	This book has a lot of time travel. Create a three-dimensional timeline to show all of the events as they happen in the book.	25		
	Weather plays a big part in advancement of the Dark in this book. Create a PowerPoint presentation about these weather changes and the weather conditions usually found in Britain.	25		
	Total number of points you are planning to earn from Side 1.	**Total points earned from Side 1:**		

Name: _____ ●

The Dark Is Rising: Side 2

Guidelines:

1. You may complete as many of the activities listed within the time period.
2. You may choose any combination of activities.
3. Your goal is 100 points. You may earn up to _____ points extra credit.
4. You may be as creative as you like within the guidelines listed below.
5. You must show your plan to your teacher by _____.
6. Activities may be turned in at any time during the working time period. They will be graded and recorded on this sheet as you continue to work, so keep it safe!

Plan to Do	Activity to Complete (Side 2: 30–40 points)	Point Value	Date Completed	Points Earned
	Will has been considered a hero. Write and perform a speech in which he discusses his thoughts about being considered a hero by other people.	30		
	Design a board game about *The Dark Is Rising* in which players answer questions while trying to obtain and join the signs of light together.	35		
	Investigate different types of fractals, including those used in this book. Create a bulletin board display that shares pictures of examples.	35		
	There are other books in *The Dark Is Rising* series. Design a commercial to convince your classmates to read the next book in the series.	35		
	Create a news report that shares the consequences for the world if Will cannot attain his goal.	40		
	This book has also been released as a movie. After reading the book, watch the movie and create a Venn diagram that shares their similarities and difference. Include a paragraph that states which format you enjoyed more and why.	40		
	Free choice: Submit your free choice proposal form for a product of your choice.			
	Total number of points you are planning to earn from Side 1.	**Total points earned from Side 1:**		
	Total number of points you are planning to earn from Side 2.	**Total points earned from Side 2:**		
		Grand Total (/100)		

I am planning to complete _____ activities that could earn up to a total of _____ points.

Teacher's initials _____ Student's signature _____

Name: _____

The Dark Is Rising

Guidelines:

1. You may complete as many of the activities listed within the time period.
2. You may choose any combination of activities.
3. Your goal is 100 points. You may earn up to _____ points extra credit.
4. You may be as creative as you like within the guidelines listed below.
5. You must show your plan to your teacher by _____.
6. Activities may be turned in at any time during the working time period. They will be graded and recorded on this sheet as you continue to work, so keep it safe!

Plan to Do	Activity to Complete	Point Value	Date Completed	Points Earned
	Complete a story map for *The Dark Is Rising*.	15		
	Will lives in a rectory. Considering the evidence found in the story, build a diorama of his home.	15		
	Create a folded quiz book for the different people Will encounters on his journey.	20		
	Design an advertisement for one of the light signs and its value to the "Old Ones."	20		
	Make a collage of modern-day items that are examples of the different signs of light. Label each item with its sign.	20		
	Weather plays a big part in the advancement of the Dark in this book. Create a three facts and a fib about these weather changes and the weather conditions usually found in Britain.	20		
	This book has a lot of time travel. Create a three-dimensional timeline to show all of the events, not in the order they occur in the book, but the order they occurred in time.	20		
	Investigate different types of fractals, including those used in this book. Create a PowerPoint presentation that shares pictures of examples.	25		
	Design a game show about *The Dark Is Rising* in which players answer questions while trying to obtain and join the signs of light together.	30		
	There are other books in *The Dark Is Rising* series. Design a commercial to convince your classmates to read the next book in the series.	30		
	Will could be considered a hero. Write and perform a speech in which he discusses his thoughts about being considered a hero by other people.	30		
	Create a news report that shares the consequences for the world if Will cannot attain his goal.	35		
	This book has also been released as a movie. After reading the book, watch the movie and create a Venn diagram that shares their similarities and difference. Include a paragraph that states which format you enjoyed more and why.	35		
	Free choice: Submit your free choice proposal form for a product of your choice.			
	Total number of points you are planning to earn.		**Total points earned:**	

I am planning to complete _____ activities that could earn up to a total of _____ points.

Teacher's initials _____ Student's signature _____

The Tale of the Mandarin Ducks

20-50-80 Menu

A beautiful duck is captured by a greedy lord who collects beautiful things. The longer he is caged, the sadder he becomes and his beauty starts to fade. The lord banishes his cage to a corner of the kitchen. Yasuko, the kitchen maid, releases him, knowing it was against the lord's wishes. For their kindness, Yasuko and Shozo, a one-eyed servant, are sentenced to death. Is there a way to save them?

Reading Objectives Covered Through These Menus and These Activities

- Students will compare one literary work with another.
- Students will make and explain inferences made from the story.
- Students will make predictions based on what is read.
- Students will show comprehension by summarizing a story.
- Students will represent textual evidence by using story maps.
- Students will analyze characters, their relationships, and their importance in the story.

Writing Objectives Covered Through These Menus and These Activities

- Students will write to express their feelings, inform, explain, describe, narrate, or reflect.
- Students will support their responses with textual evidence.
- Students will exhibit voice in their writing.

Materials Needed by Students for Completion

- *The Tale of the Mandarin Ducks* by Katherine Paterson
- Poster board or large white paper
- Microsoft PowerPoint or other slideshow software ■
- DVD or VHS recorder (for commercials ●, videos)
- Recycled materials (for models) ▲
- Coat hangers (for mobiles) ▲
- String (for mobiles) ▲
- Blank index cards (for mobiles) ▲
- Magazines (for collages) ▲

Special Notes on the Modifications of These Menus

- If needed, further modifications can be made to a 20-50-80 menu based on the needs of your students. The easiest modification is altering the point goal from 100; lowering or raising the goal on a menu by 10 (or 20) points is appropriate if additional modification up or down is needed.

Special Notes on the Use of These Menus

- These menus give students the opportunity to create a video and commercial ●. Although students enjoy producing their own videos, there often are difficulties obtaining the equipment and scheduling the use of a video recorder. This activity can be modified by allowing students to act out the product (like a play) or, if students have the technology, allowing them to produce a webcam version of their presentation.
- The triangle menu ▲ asks students to use recycled materials to create their model. This does not mean only plastic and paper; instead, students should focus on using materials in new ways. It works well if a box is started for "recycled" contributions at the beginning of the school year. That way, students always have access to these types of materials.
- The square menu ■ allows students to create a bulletin board display. Some classrooms may only have one bulletin board, so the teacher can divide the board into sections, or additional classroom wall or hall space can be sectioned off for the creation of these displays. Students can plan their display based on the amount of space they are assigned.

Time Frame

- 1–2 weeks—Students are given a menu as the unit is started, and the teacher discusses all of the product options on the menu. As the different options are discussed, students will choose the activities they are most interested in completing so they meet their goal of 100 points. As the lessons progress through the week(s), the teacher and students refer back to the menu options associated with the content being taught.
- 1–2 days—The teacher chooses an activity from the menus to use with the entire class.

Suggested Forms

- All-purpose rubric
- Student presentation rubric
- Proposal form for point-based projects

The Tale of the Mandarin Ducks

Directions: Choose at least two activities from the options below. The activities must total 100 points. Place a checkmark next to each box to show which activities you will complete. All activities must be completed by: _____.

20 points

❒ Create a model of the hut where Yasuko and Shozo slept in the woods.

❒ Design a character mobile with each of the characters on it. Under each character, place words to describe him or her.

50 points

❒ Create a collage of items that the Lord may have collected. Label each item with the reason why he would have valued it.

❒ Make a poster that shares information about the samurai and their importance in Japanese culture.

❒ Create a brochure to share information about Mandarin ducks. Include information you find interesting.

❒ Free choice: Submit a proposal form for a product of your choice.

80 points

❒ Select another folktale that you feel is similar to *The Tale of the Mandarin Ducks*. Use a Venn diagram to compare the two works.

❒ Storytelling is very important in this culture. Pretend that you are Shozo and record a video that tells your children the tale of the Mandarin ducks.

The Tale of the Mandarin Ducks

Directions: Choose at least two activities from the options below. The activities must total 100 points. Place a checkmark next to each box to show which activities you will complete. All activities must be completed by: _____.

20 points

❏ Create a bulletin board display to share information about Mandarin ducks. Include information you find interesting.

❏ Shozo was once a great samurai. Design a poster that shares information about the samurai and their importance in Japanese culture.

50 points

❏ Select another folktale that you feel is similar to *The Tale of the Mandarin Ducks*. Use a Venn diagram to compare the two works.

❏ Design a commercial for a present-day product that you think the Lord would like to add to his collection.

❏ Do you believe in putting animals in cages? Prepare a speech that shares the reasons behind your view on this topic.

❏ Free choice: Submit a proposal form for a product of your choice.

80 points

❏ Storytelling is very important in this culture. Pretend that you are Shozo and record a video that tells your children the tale of the Mandarin ducks.

❏ Write a children's book that shares this story from the point of view of the duck, the drake's mate.

The Tale of the Mandarin Ducks

Directions: Choose at least two activities from the options below. The activities must total 100 points. Place a checkmark next to each box to show which activities you will complete. All activities must be completed by: _____.

20 points

❏ Create a bulletin board display to share information about Mandarin ducks. Be sure to include information on their habitats and where they are located in the wild.

❏ Shozo was once a great samurai. Design a PowerPoint presentation that shares information about the samurai and their importance in Japanese culture.

50 points

❏ Write a children's book that shares this story from the point of view of the duck, the drake's mate.

❏ Select another folktale that you feel is similar to *The Tale of the Mandarin Ducks*. Write a short paragraph explaining why you selected the folktale and use a Venn diagram to compare the two works.

❏ Storytelling is very important in this culture. Pretend that you are Shozo and record a video in which you tell your children and grandchildren how a Mandarin duck changed your life.

❏ Free choice: Submit a proposal form for a product of your choice.

80 points

❏ Consider what may have happened to the Lord after his two servants went with the messenger and write a second chapter to the book that focuses on the Lord's life after their departure.

❏ After identifying the message of this folktale, perform a speech, not specifically about the book, but about the importance of the message and how the message applies to others your age.

Roll of Thunder, Hear My Cry

Three-Topic List Menu

This story chronicles of the lives of the Logan family as they struggle to earn a living on their farm in Mississippi during the Depression. When the Wallace family, the family who owns the only store in town, takes justice into their own hands, Mr. Logan devises a plan to try and address the situation. Things, however, may not turn out as everyone hopes they will.

Reading Objectives Covered Through These Menus and These Activities

- Students will represent textual evidence and use it to prove conclusions.
- Students will compare one literary work with another.
- Students will make and explain inferences made from the story.
- Students will make predictions based on what is read.
- Students will show comprehension by summarizing a story.
- Students will represent textual evidence by using story maps.
- Students will analyze characters, their relationships, and their importance in the story.
- Students will recognize and analyze story plot and problem resolution.

Writing Objectives Covered Through These Menus and These Activities

- Students will write to express their feelings, inform, explain, describe, narrate, entertain, influence, persuade, or reflect.
- Students will support their responses with textual evidence.
- Students will use vivid language.
- Students will revise drafts.

Materials Needed by Students for Completion

- *Roll of Thunder, Hear My Cry* by Mildred D. Taylor
- *Song of the Trees* by Mildred D. Taylor ◼
- Poster board or large white paper
- Materials for museum exhibit ◼
- Microsoft PowerPoint or other slideshow software ● ◼
- Aluminum foil (for quiz board) ◼
- Wires (for quiz board) ◼
- Scrapbooking materials ◼

- DVD or VHS recorder (for news reports)
- Graph paper or Internet access (for crossword puzzles)
- Blank index cards (for trading cards ▲ ●, concentration cards ▲)
- Story map ▲ ●
- Magazines (for collages) ● ■

Special Notes on the Modifications of These Menus

- Because a List menu is a point-based menu, it is easy to provide additional modifications by simply changing the point goal for those students who need it. The bottom of each menu has a short contract that can be used to record any changes in point goals.

Special Notes on the Use of These Menus

- These menus give students the opportunity to create a news report. Although students enjoy producing their own videos, there often are difficulties obtaining the equipment and scheduling the use of a video recorder. This activity can be modified by allowing students to act out the product (like a play) or, if students have the technology, allowing them to produce a webcam version of their presentation.
- The circle and square menus ● ■ allow students to create a bulletin board display. Some classrooms may only have one bulletin board, so the teacher can divide the board into sections, or additional classroom wall or hall space can be sectioned off for the creation of these displays. Students can plan their display based on the amount of space they are assigned.
- The square menu ■ provides the opportunity for students to create a quiz board. A student-friendly informational sheet that offers the steps for constructing their own quiz board is available at http://www.cesiscience.org/attachments/article/100/QuizBoardDirections.pdf.

Time Frame

- 1–2 weeks—Students are given a menu as the unit is started, and the guidelines and point expectations are discussed. Students usually will need to earn 100 points for 100%, although there is an opportunity for extra credit if the teacher would like to use another target number. Because this menu covers three topics in depth, the teacher may choose to only go over the options for the topic being covered first; the students place check marks in the boxes next to the activities they are most interested in completing. As instruction continues, additional explanation of the new topic activities can be provided. Once students have access to the entire menu, teachers will need to set aside a few moments to sign the agreement at the bottom of the page with each student. As activities are completed by students, they will be submitted to the teacher for grading.

- 1–2 days—The teacher chooses an activity from the menus to use with the entire class.

Suggested Forms

- All-purpose rubric
- Student-taught lesson rubric ▲ ●
- Student presentation rubric
- Proposal form for point-based products

Roll of Thunder, Hear My Cry

Guidelines:

1. You may complete as many of the activities listed as you can within the time period.
2. You may choose any combination of activities, but **must** complete at least one activity from each topic area.
3. Your goal is 100 points. You may earn up to _____ points extra credit.
4. You may be as creative as you like within the guidelines listed below.
5. You must share your plan with your teacher by _____.
6. Activities may be turned in at any time during the working time period. They will be graded and recorded on this sheet as you continue to work, so keep it safe!

Topic	Plan to Do	Activity to Complete	Point Value	Date Completed	Points Earned
Background Information		Make a drawing that shows how a sharecropping farm might be organized.	15		
		Make a list of five things that happen in the story that are true based on history.	20		
		Mildred Taylor has written other books about the Logan family; read another of the books in the Logan series. Retell a scene from the book you chose to read.	25		
		Use a Venn diagram to compare the life of a sharecropper with a farmer who owns his own land.	25		
		Prepare a student-taught lesson that teaches your classmates about the Great Depression.	30		
Characters		Create a set of concentration cards that allows users to match the names of the characters with a drawing of each.	15		
		Design a set of trading cards for the members of the Logan family.	20		
		Use a mind map to analyze the characters in the story that are not part of the Logan family. Record character traits for each character in the mind map.	25		
		Come to class as one of the characters in this story. Tell your classmates about the most important event in the story.	30		
Plot		Complete another student's crossword puzzle.	15		
		Create a flipbook to share at least four important events in the story. Put the event on the top flap and what caused each event inside each flap.	20		
		Complete a story map for *Roll of Thunder, Hear My Cry*.	25		
		Make a crossword puzzle for *Roll of Thunder, Hear My Cry*.	25		
		Design a timeline that shares the important events in the story as they take place.	30		
Analysis of Roll of Thunder, Hear My Cry		Create a T-chart to show which characters are antagonists and which are protagonists in this story. Write a sentence for each character.	15		
		Make a poster with examples of written dialect taken from the story.	20		
		Make a new book cover for *Roll of Thunder, Hear My Cry*.	25		
		Record a news report that shares what happens when T.J. is drug from his home by the White men.	35		
Any		**Free choice**: Submit your free choice proposal form for a product of your choice.			
		Total number of points you are planning to earn.	**Total points earned:**		

I am planning to complete _____ activities that could earn up to a total of _____ points.

Teacher's initials _____ Student's signature _____

Name: _____

Roll of Thunder, Hear My Cry: Side 1

Guidelines:

1. You may complete as many of the activities listed as you can within the time period.
2. You may choose any combination of activities, but **must** complete at least one activity from each topic area.
3. Your goal is 100 points. You may earn up to _____ points extra credit.
4. You may be as creative as you like within the guidelines listed below.
5. You must share your plan with your teacher by _____.
6. Activities may be turned in at any time during the working time period. They will be graded and recorded on this sheet as you continue to work, so keep it safe!

Topic	Plan to Do	Activity to Complete	Point Value	Date Completed	Points Earned
Background Information		Use a Venn diagram to compare the life of a sharecropper with a farmer who owns his own land.	15		
		Design a bulletin board display that shares information about the Great Depression, its cause, and its impact on people's lives.	20		
		The Logan family organizes a boycott in the story. Prepare a PowerPoint presentation that shares information on this strategy and how it can be effective.	25		
		Prepare a student-taught lesson that teaches your classmates important historical information that will help them better understand the events in the story.	30		
		Mildred Taylor has written other books about the Logan family; read another of the books in the Logan series. Create an advertisement for the book you have read to convince your classmates to read the book.	30		
Characters		Make a folded quiz book to test your classmates on their knowledge of the different characters.	15		
		Design a set of trading cards for the different characters in the story.	15		
		Use a mind map to analyze the different characters. Record character traits for each and include at least one quote about each that supports the traits you have chosen for that character.	20		
		Come to class as one of the characters in this story. Be prepared to talk about how you feel about at least two of the events from the story.	25		
		Write a newspaper article about prejudice. In your article, be sure you provide information from your interview with Cassie about her thoughts on the matter.	30		
		Total number of points you are planning to earn from Side 1.		**Total points earned from Side 1:**	

Name: _____

Roll of Thunder, Hear My Cry: Side 2

Guidelines:

1. You may complete as many of the activities listed as you can within the time period.
2. You may choose any combination of activities, but **must** complete at least one activity from each topic area.
3. Your goal is 100 points. You may earn up to _____ points extra credit.
4. You may be as creative as you like within the guidelines listed below.
5. You must share your plan with your teacher by _____.
6. Activities may be turned in at any time during the working time period. They will be graded and recorded on this sheet as you continue to work, so keep it safe!

Topic	Plan to Do	Activity to Complete	Point Value	Date Completed	Points Earned
Plot		Complete another student's crossword puzzle.	10		
		Create a flipbook to share at least six important events in the story and what caused each to take place.	15		
		Complete a story map for this story.	20		
		Make a crossword puzzle for *Roll of Thunder, Hear My Cry*.	20		
		Design a three-dimensional timeline that shares the important events in the story as they take place.	25		
Analysis of Roll of Thunder, Hear My Cry		Make a collage of quotes from this story with examples of written dialect. Include a "translation" for each.	15		
		Make a windowpane that gives examples of how each character is affected by injustice.	15		
		Make a book cover for *Roll of Thunder, Hear My Cry*.	20		
		Foreshadowing is used frequently in this novel. Use a chart to record at least eight examples found in the story and the events to which they lead.	25		
		Record a news report that covers the events of the Third Sunday in August.	30		
Any		**Free choice:** Submit your free choice proposal form for a product of your choice.			
		Total number of points you are planning to earn from Side 1.		**Total points earned from Side 1:**	
		Total number of points you are planning to earn from Side 2.		**Total points earned from Side 2:**	
				Grand Total (/100)	

I am planning to complete _____ activities that could earn up to a total of _____ points.

Teacher's initials _____ Student's signature _____

Name: _____

Roll of Thunder, Hear My Cry: Side 1

Guidelines:

1. You may complete as many of the activities listed as you can within the time period.
2. You may choose any combination of activities, but **must** complete at least one activity from each topic area.
3. Your goal is 100 points. You may earn up to _____ points extra credit.
4. You may be as creative as you like within the guidelines listed below.
5. You must share your plan with your teacher by _____.
6. Activities may be turned in at any time during the working time period. They will be graded and recorded on this sheet as you continue to work, so keep it safe!

Topic	Plan to Do	Activity to Complete	Point Value	Date Completed	Points Earned
Background Information		Use a Venn diagram to compare the life of a sharecropper with a farmer who owns his own land.	10		
		Design a bulletin board display that shares significant historical events that took place in the United States during the time period covered in this story.	15		
		Research the practice of sharecropping. Create a museum exhibit to teach others about its advantages and disadvantages.	20		
		The Logan family organizes a boycott in the story. Prepare a PowerPoint presentation to share information on this tactic. Include at least two occasions in history when it has been used successfully.	25		
		Mildred Taylor has written other books about the Logan family. Read *Song of the Trees* and write an essay on how the characters have changed in *Roll of Thunder, Hear My Cry*.	30		
Characters		Make a quiz board to test your classmates on their knowledge of the different characters. Be creative in your descriptions and questions.	15		
		Make a windowpane in which you list each character and then write the name of a character from a book, movie, or cartoon who has the same traits. Include a sentence to explain how they are similar.	15		
		Use a mind map to analyze the different characters. Record character traits for each and include at least two quotes about each that support the traits you have chosen for that character.	20		
		Big Ma shares stories with the children. She talks about her family and their experiences. Create a scrapbook to document the events she discusses.	25		
		Record a news report about prejudice. In your report, you should interview at least two of the characters who will have differing views on the topic.	30		
		Total number of points you are planning to earn from Side 1.		**Total points earned from Side 1:**	

Name: _____ ■

Roll of Thunder, Hear My Cry: Side 2

Guidelines:

1. You may complete as many of the activities listed as you can within the time period.
2. You may choose any combination of activities, but **must** complete at least one activity from each topic area.
3. Your goal is 100 points. You may earn up to _____ points extra credit.
4. You may be as creative as you like within the guidelines listed below.
5. You must share your plan with your teacher by _____.
6. Activities may be turned in at any time during the working time period. They will be graded and recorded on this sheet as you continue to work, so keep it safe!

Topic	Plan to Do	Activity to Complete	Point Value	Date Completed	Points Earned
Plot		Create a flipbook to share at least eight important events in the story and what caused each to take place.	15		
		Make a crossword puzzle for *Roll of Thunder, Hear My Cry*.	15		
		Design a three-dimensional timeline that shares the important events in the story as they take place. Include at least two events before the story begins and two that take place after it has ended.	20		
		Although not part of the Logan family, T.J. causes changes to the plot of this story. Prepare a speech that defends the idea that T.J. is one of the most important characters in the story.	25		
		Determine the turning point of the story and consider how it may change the story if the outcome was different. Rewrite the rest of the story based on this new outcome.	30		
Analysis of *Roll of Thunder, Hear My Cry*		Make a collage of quotes from this story as well as two other stories with examples of written dialect. Include a "translation" for each.	10		
		Almost all of the characters experience injustice in one manner or another in this story. Design a poster that gives examples of how each character is affected by injustice. Include a quote for each situation.	15		
		Foreshadowing is used frequently in this novel. Use a chart to record one example of foreshadowing for each chapter and the event to which it leads.	25		
		Write a newspaper article that covers the events of the Third Sunday in August.	25		
		Write an essay that addresses the significance of the title to this story. Include quotes as well as explanations that show its importance.	30		
Any		**Free choice:** Submit your free choice proposal form for a product of your choice.			
		Total number of points you are planning to earn from Side 1.		**Total points earned from Side 1:**	
		Total number of points you are planning to earn from Side 2.		**Total points earned from Side 2:**	
				Grand Total (/100)	

I am planning to complete _____ activities that could earn up to a total of _____ points.

Teacher's initials _____ Student's signature _____

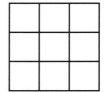

A Wrinkle in Time

Meal Menu ▲ and
Tic-Tac-Toe Menu ● ■

After her scientist father has been missing for a year, Meg Murry is told he has been imprisoned by an evil force on another planet. The only way she will be able to save him is to travel to the planet through a tesseract, or wrinkle in time and space. Meg, her little brother Charles Wallace, and friend Calvin embark on the journey with the help of the Mrs W's, and other creatures they meet along way. Even if they can rescue Mr. Murry, will all of the heroes make it back unscathed?

Reading Objectives Covered Through These Menus and These Activities

- Students will represent textual evidence and use it to prove conclusions.
- Students will make and explain inferences made from the story.
- Students will make predictions based on what is read.
- Students will show comprehension by summarizing a story.
- Students will represent textual evidence by using story maps.
- Students will analyze characters, their relationships, and their importance in the story.
- Students will recognize and analyze story plot and problem resolution.

Writing Objectives Covered Through These Menus and These Activities

- Students will write to express their feelings, inform, explain, describe, narrate, entertain, persuade, reflect, or problem solve.
- Students will support their responses with textual evidence.
- Students will exhibit voice in their writing.

Materials Needed by Students for Completion

- *A Wrinkle in Time* by Madeleine L'Engle
- Poster board or large white paper
- DVD or VHS recorder (for commercials ▲ ●, news reports ■, video ■)
- Scrapbooking materials
- Magazines (for collages) ■
- Story map ▲
- Coat hangers (for mobiles) ▲
- String (for mobiles) ▲
- Blank index cards (for mobiles, trading cards) ▲

Special Notes on the Modifications of These Menus

- This topic has two different menu formats: The Meal menu (▲) and Tic-Tac-Toe (● ■) menu. The Meal menu is specifically selected for the triangle option as it easily allows the menu to be broken into manageable bits; the different meals separate the page, making it less daunting for special needs students. The space between the meals makes it easy for the teacher to cut the menu as needed based on the comfort level of the students. If it is the first time choice is being introduced, then the children may receive only the strip of the top breakfast options. Then, when they have finished one of those options, they can receive a strip of lunches and finally the enrichment-level dinner and dessert activities. After students have grown more accustomed to making choices, the menu might be cut just once after the lunch options, so students can select a breakfast and a lunch and submit them to the teacher. Then, they can choose from the dinner strip they receive. The ultimate goal would be for students to have all nine options at once and not be overwhelmed.

Special Notes on the Use of These Menus

- These menus give students the opportunity to create news reports ■, videos ■, and commercials ▲ ●. Although students enjoy producing their own videos, there often are difficulties obtaining the equipment and scheduling the use of a video recorder. This activity can be modified by allowing students to act out the product (like a play) or, if students have the technology, allowing them to produce a webcam version of their presentation.

Time Frame

- 2–3 weeks—Students are given a menu as the unit is started. As the teacher presents lessons throughout the week, he or she should refer back to the menu options associated with that content. The teacher will go over all of the options for that content and have students place check marks in the boxes that represent the activities they are most interested in completing. As students choose activities, they should complete a column or a row. When students complete this pattern, they have completed one activity from each content area, learning style, or level of Bloom's revised taxonomy, depending on the design of the menu.
- 1 week—At the start of the unit, the teacher chooses the three activities he or she feels are most valuable for students. Stations can be set up in the classroom. These three activities are available for student choice throughout the week as regular instruction takes place.

- 1–2 days—The teacher chooses an activity from the menus to use with the entire class.

Suggested Forms

- All-purpose rubric
- Student presentation rubric
- Free-choice proposal form

A Wrinkle in Time

Directions: Choose one activity each for breakfast, lunch, and dinner. Dessert is an activity you can choose to do after you have finished your other meals. All products must be completed by: _____.

Breakfast

❑ Create a picture dictionary for at least 15 "new to you" vocabulary words from our story.

❑ Complete a story map for *A Wrinkle in Time*.

❑ Make a mobile that shares information about this book and its author.

Lunch

❑ Which characters are you most and least like? Use a Venn diagram to compare yourself with one of the characters in our story.

❑ Create a set of trading cards for the different creatures and characters found in our story.

❑ Design a children's book with drawings of all of the creatures and information about where they live.

Dinner

❑ Create a scrapbook to share Meg's experiences on the different planets.

❑ When they arrive on Uriel, the children encounter creatures that produce beautiful songs. Select a song that you think these creatures would enjoy performing and share it with your classmates.

❑ Free choice: Submit a free choice proposal about the events in *A Wrinkle in Time* to your teacher for approval.

Dessert

❑ Come to school as Mrs Whatsit. Be prepared to discuss your unique qualities and how you help the children on their quest.

❑ Record a travel commercial to convince others to visit the planet that you think is the best.

Name: _____

A Wrinkle in Time

Directions: Check the boxes you plan to complete. They should form a tic-tac-toe across or down. All products are due by: _____.

☐ **Who Am I?**	☐ **The Journey**	☐ **The Analysis**
Which characters are you most and least like? Use a Venn diagram to compare yourself with one of the characters in our story.	When they arrive on Uriel, the children encounter creatures that produce beautiful songs. Write and perform a song that you think these creatures would enjoy performing.	Mrs Whatsit makes many quote-worthy comments. Select the quote you think is most meaningful to you and create a poster that shares the quote and examples of why it is important for teenagers to remember it.
☐ **The Analysis**	☐ **Free Choice:** *One of the Characters Found in* A Wrinkle in Time (Fill out your proposal form before beginning the free choice!)	☐ **The Journey**
Consider the IT and its impact on its planet. Record a commercial to convince others that living on Camazotz is not that different from life as a teenager.		Create a scrapbook for Meg's experiences on the different planets. Be sure and include the unique qualities of their inhabitants as well as of the planets themselves.
☐ **The Journey**	☐ **The Analysis**	☐ **The Mrs W's**
Keep a journal for Meg to document her experiences with the Black Thing. Begin your journal when Meg reaches Camazotz.	The author uses very specific vocabulary throughout the story. Create a picture dictionary for at least 15 vocabulary words that describe a character or creature.	Although the Mrs W's are often referred to as a group, each is unique. Come to school as the Mrs W you find most interesting. Be prepared to discuss your unique qualities and how you help the children on their quest.

A Wrinkle in Time

Directions: Check the boxes you plan to complete. They should form a tic-tac-toe across or down. All products are due by: _____.

☐ **The Mrs W's**	☐ **The Journey**	☐ **The Analysis**
Although the Mrs W's are often referred to as a group, each is unique. Come to school as the Mrs W you find most interesting. Be prepared to discuss your unique qualities and how you help the children on their quest.	At first, the children found communication difficult with the various creatures they encountered. Select one of these different methods that the creatures use to communicate and prepare a product that communicates a message using the method you have selected.	Scientists have researched and debated the possibility of a "wrinkle in time," or time travel itself. Research what others have said about this phenomenon and write a research paper that shares the information you have discovered. Be sure to include a bibliography!
☐ **The Analysis**	☐ **Free Choice:** *One of the Characters Found in* **A Wrinkle in Time** (Fill out your proposal form before beginning the free choice!)	☐ **The Journey**
According to the information in the story, Earth has also been affected by the Black Thing. Perform a news report that shares this information and the evidence that the Black Thing is here.		Create a scrapbook for Meg's experiences on the different planets. Be sure and include the unique qualities of their inhabitants as well as of the planets themselves.
☐ **The Journey**	☐ **The Analysis**	☐ **Who Am I?**
Keep a journal for Meg to document her experiences. It should begin the night that Mrs Whatsit came to visit her and continue until the resolution of the story.	The author uses very specific vocabulary throughout the story. Create a mural-sized collage of words and quotes that have significance to the tone and mood. Label each item with how it impacts the tone or mood.	Which characters are you most and least like? Record a video in which you compare yourself to each of the characters. Your video should be more than just you talking; incorporate your experiences and life events.

"Eleven"

20-50-80 Menu

In this short story, we meet Rachel on her birthday as she ponders turning 11. Although birthdays are usually happy occasions, that is not the case for Rachel. After dealing with a mix-up concerning an unclaimed sweater at school, Rachel has a very upsetting birthday.

Reading Objectives Covered Through These Menus and These Activities

- Students will make and explain inferences made from the story.
- Students will make predictions based on what is read.
- Students will show comprehension by summarizing a story.
- Students will represent textual evidence by using story maps.
- Students will recognize and analyze story plot and problem resolution.

Writing Objectives Covered Through These Menus and These Activities

- Students will write to express their feelings, inform, explain, or describe.
- Students will support their responses with textual evidence.
- Students will exhibit voice in their writing.

Materials Needed by Students for Completion

- "Eleven" by Sandra Cisneros
- Poster board or large white paper
- Story Analysis Cube template ■
- Character Cube template ▲ ●
- Recycled materials (for dioramas) ▲

Special Notes on the Modifications of These Menus

- If needed, further modifications can be made to a 20-50-80 menu based on the needs of your students. The easiest modification is altering the point goal from 100; lowering or raising the goal on a menu by 10 (or 20) points is appropriate if additional modification up or down is needed.

Time Frame

- 1–2 weeks—Students are given a menu as the unit is started, and the teacher discusses all of the product options on the menu. As the different options are discussed, students will choose the activities they are most interested in completing so they meet their goal of 100 points. As the lessons progress through the week(s), the teacher and students refer back to the menu options associated with the content being taught.

- 1–2 days—The teacher chooses an activity from the menus to use with the entire class.

Suggested Forms

- All-purpose rubric
- Student presentation rubric
- Proposal form for point-based projects

"Eleven"

Directions: Choose at least two activities from the options below. The activities must total 100 points. Place a checkmark next to each box to show which activities you will complete. All activities must be completed by: _____.

20 points

❑ Design a birthday card you could give Rachel for her birthday.

❑ Based on Rachel's description, make a drawing of the red sweater.

50 points

❑ Complete a character cube for "Eleven."

❑ Use a Venn diagram to compare your last birthday with Rachel's birthday.

❑ Make a diorama of Rachel with the red sweater on her desk.

❑ Free choice: Submit a proposal form for a product of your choice.

80 points

❑ Thinking back on all of your birthdays, have they all been exactly what you expected? Retell a story about the events that took place on one of your birthdays.

❑ Conduct a survey in which you ask your classmates about whether birthdays are always happy days. Use a poster to present the information you gathered.

"Eleven"

Directions: Choose at least two activities from the options below. The activities must total 100 points. Place a checkmark next to each box to show which activities you will complete. All activities must be completed by: _____.

20 points
❏ Design a birthday card you could give Rachel for her birthday.
❏ Complete the "Eleven" character cube.

50 points
❏ Use a Venn diagram to compare your last birthday with Rachel's birthday.
❏ Make a mind map that shows occasions when, like Rachel, you have been all of the ages before your current age.
❏ Conduct a survey in which you ask your classmates about whether birthdays are always happy days. Present your data using graphs on a poster.
❏ Free choice: Submit a proposal form for a product of your choice.

80 points
❏ Thinking back on all of your birthdays, have they all been exactly what you expected? Write a children's book about the events that took place on one of your birthdays.
❏ If Rachel could have changed something about her day, what would it have been? Rewrite the story from this point with the new ending.

"Eleven"

Directions: Choose at least two activities from the options below. The activities must total 100 points. Place a checkmark next to each box to show which activities you will complete. All activities must be completed by: _____.

20 points

☐ Design a birthday card you could give Rachel for her birthday.

☐ Use a Venn diagram to compare your last birthday with Rachel's birthday.

50 points

☐ Make a mind map that shows occasions when, like Rachel, you have been all of the ages before your current age.

☐ Complete a story analysis cube for "Eleven."

☐ If Rachel could have changed something about her day, what would it have been? Rewrite the story from this point with the new ending.

☐ Turn "Eleven" into a play. Perform the play for your classmates.

80 points

☐ Thinking back on all of your birthdays, have they all been exactly what you expected? Write a children's book about the events that took place on one of your birthdays.

☐ Free choice: Submit a proposal form for a product of your choice.

"Eleven" Character Cube

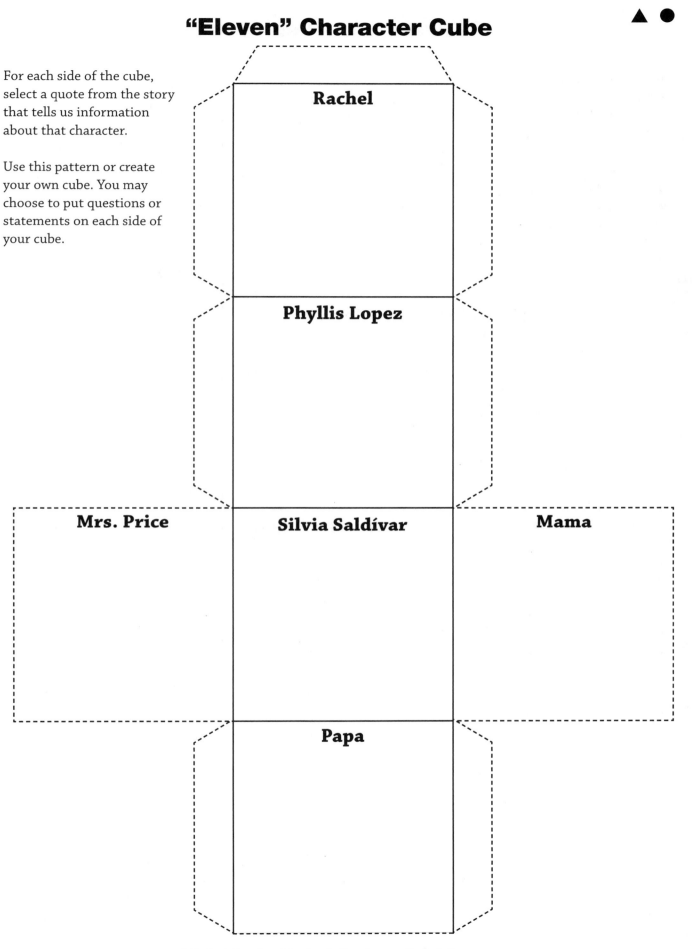

For each side of the cube, select a quote from the story that tells us information about that character.

Use this pattern or create your own cube. You may choose to put questions or statements on each side of your cube.

Rachel

Phyllis Lopez

Mrs. Price

Silvia Saldívar

Mama

Papa

"Eleven" Analysis Cube

■

Provide examples of each literary device on each side of the cube. For each example, include a quote.

Use this pattern or create your own cube. You may choose to put questions or statements on each side of your cube.

Imagery

Simile

| **Tone** | **Characterization** | **Point of View** |

Inference

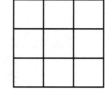

Dragonwings

Meal Menu ▲ and
Tic-Tac-Toe Menu ● ■

Having never met his father, Moon Shadow was excited when he was given the chance to go to "the Land of the Golden Mountain," San Francisco, to live with him. Although a master kite maker in China, Moon Shadow's father, Windrider, now works in a laundry. Both father and son share experiences in their quest to achieve their dreams. Will they be able to find happiness?

Reading Objectives Covered Through These Menus and These Activities

- Students will represent textual evidence and use it to prove conclusions.
- Students will compare one literary work with another.
- Students will make and explain inferences made from the story.
- Students will make predictions based on what is read.
- Students will show comprehension by summarizing a story.
- Students will represent textual evidence by using story maps.
- Students will analyze characters, their relationships, and their importance in the story.
- Students will recognize and analyze story plot and problem resolution.

Writing Objectives Covered Through These Menus and These Activities

- Students will write to express their feelings, inform, explain, describe, narrate, or entertain.
- Students will support their responses with textual evidence.
- Students will exhibit voice in their writing.

Materials Needed by Students for Completion

- *Dragonwings* by Laurence Yep
- Coat hangers (for mobiles)
- String (for mobiles)
- Blank index cards (for mobiles)
- Microsoft PowerPoint or other slideshow software ● ■
- DVD or VHS recorder (for documentary) ● ■
- Poster board or large white paper
- Scrapbooking materials ●
- Recycled materials (for models, dioramas) ▲
- Story map ▲

Special Notes on the Modifications of These Menus

- This topic has two different menu formats: the Meal menu (▲) and Tic-Tac-Toe (● ■) menu. The Meal menu is specifically selected for the triangle option as it easily allows the menu to be broken into manageable bits; the different meals separate the page, making it less daunting for special needs students. The space between the meals makes it easy for the teacher to cut the menu as needed based on the comfort level of the students. If it is the first time choice is being introduced, then the children may receive only the strip of the top breakfast options. Then, when they have finished one of those options, they can receive a strip of lunches and finally the enrichment-level dinner and dessert activities. After students have grown more accustomed to making choices, the menu might be cut just once after the lunch options, so students can select a breakfast and a lunch and submit them to the teacher. Then, they can choose from the dinner strip they receive. The ultimate goal would be for students to have all nine options at once and not be overwhelmed.

Special Notes on the Use of This Menu

- The circle and square ● ■ menus give students the opportunity to create a video documentary. Although students enjoy producing their own videos, there often are difficulties obtaining the equipment and scheduling the use of a video recorder. This activity can be modified by allowing students to act out the product (like a play) or, if students have the technology, allowing them to produce a webcam version of their presentation.
- The triangle and circle menus ▲ ● ask students to use recycled materials to create their models and dioramas. This does not mean only plastic and paper; instead, students should focus on using materials in new ways. It works well if a box is started for "recycled" contributions at the beginning of the school year. That way, students always have access to these types of materials.
- The circle menu ● allows students to create a bulletin board display. Some classrooms may only have one bulletin board, so the teacher can divide the board into sections, or additional classroom wall or hall space can be sectioned off for the creation of these displays. Students can plan their display based on the amount of space they are assigned.

Time Frame

- 2–3 weeks—Students are given a menu as the unit is started. As the teacher presents lessons throughout the week, he or she should refer back to the menu options associated with that content. The teacher will go over all of the options for that content and have students place check marks in the boxes that represent the activities they are most interested in completing. As students choose activities, they should complete a column or a row. When students complete this pattern, they have completed one activity from each content area, learning style, or level of Bloom's revised taxonomy, depending on the design of the menu.

- 1 week—At the start of the unit, the teacher chooses the three activities he or she feels are most valuable for students. Stations can be set up in the classroom. These three activities are available for student choice throughout the week as regular instruction takes place.
- 1–2 days—The teacher chooses an activity from the menus to use with the entire class.

Suggested Forms

- All-purpose rubric
- Student presentation rubric
- Student-taught lesson rubric ● ■
- Free-choice proposal form

Dragonwings

Directions: Choose one activity each for breakfast, lunch, and dinner. Dessert is an activity you can choose to do after you have finished your other meals. All products must be completed by: _____.

Breakfast

☐ Design a character mobile for the characters in *Dragonwings*. Include one quote for each character.

☐ Complete a story map for *Dragonwings*.

☐ Make a Venn diagram to compare two characters in the story.

Lunch

☐ Create a model of the Company of Peach Orchard Vow.

☐ Make an advertisement to bring more customers to the company where Windrider works.

☐ Design a diorama of the most exciting scene in the story.

Dinner

☐ Make a drawing that shares the different reasons people leave their homes to move to other countries.

☐ The story ends in 1910. Tell a story that shares what happens to our characters in the year following Windrider's return to the United States.

☐ Dragons are viewed differently by the characters in this story. Find a children's book that shows a dragon in the way Windrider views them. Share the book with your classmates.

Dessert

☐ The Tang people believe that a person can change his or her name as he or she grows up and changes. Make a poster to share what your name would be based on Tang tradition and why it fits you.

☐ Free choice: Submit a free choice proposal about *Dragonwings* to your teacher for approval.

Dragonwings

Directions: Check the boxes you plan to complete. They should form a tic-tac-toe across or down. All products are due by: _____.

☐ **The Characters** Design a character trait mobile for the characters in *Dragonwings*. Be sure and include at least two quotes for each character that support the trait you have selected.	☐ **San Francisco** Make a bulletin board display that shares information and photographs of the major historical events that took place in San Francisco between 1903 and 1910.	☐ **Immigrants** Research the immigration between China and the United States during the early 1900s. Design a PowerPoint presentation to share your findings. Be sure and include historical photos.
☐ **The Wright Brothers** The Wright brothers had many accomplishments. Create a class lesson to teach others about the Wright brothers and their work.	☐ **Free Choice:** ***On the Characters of* Dragonwings** (Fill out your proposal form before beginning the free choice!)	☐ **The Next Chapter** The story ends in 1910. Write a story that shares what happens to our characters in the next year following Windrider's return to the United States.
☐ **A Name** The Tang people believe that a person can change his or her name as he or she grows up and changes. Design a scrapbook for your family members to share what their names would be based on Tang tradition and why these names fit them.	☐ **Culture** Throughout the story, Moon Shadow has certain perceptions about the people of San Francisco. Create a video documentary that shares how these views change over time.	☐ **Dragons** Dragons are viewed differently by the characters in this story. Find two children's books that show a dragon in the way Windrider views them and the way Mrs. Whitlaw views them. Make a diorama showing the differences between the two.

Name: _____

Dragonwings

Directions: Check the boxes you plan to complete. They should form a tic-tac-toe across or down. All products are due by: _____.

☐ **The Characters**	☐ **Through Another's Eyes**	☐ **Immigrants**
Design a character trait mobile for the characters in *Dragonwings*. Be sure and include at least three quotes for each character that support the trait you have selected.	Select a character who is not in the Company. Write an essay that describes Moon Shadow as they see him. Include at least three quotes in your essay to support your view.	Research the immigration patterns between other countries and the United States from 1800 to present day. Design a PowerPoint presentation to share your findings. Be sure and include historical photos.
☐ **The Wright Brothers**	☐ **Free Choice:** *On the Characters of* **Dragonwings** (Fill out your proposal form before beginning the free choice!)	☐ **The Next Chapter**
The Wright brothers had many accomplishments and failures. Create a class lesson to teach others about their goals, dreams, and persistence of the Wright brothers and their work.		The story ends in 1910. Write a story that shares what happens to our characters in the 5 years following the ending of the story.
☐ **Immigration**	☐ **Culture**	☐ **Dragons**
Select another novel in which immigration plays a significant role. After reading that novel, use a Venn diagram to compare the main character in the novel's views of his or her new home with Moon Shadow's views of San Francisco.	Throughout the story, Moon Shadow has certain perceptions about the people of San Francisco. Create a video documentary that shares the origins of his views and how they change as the book progresses.	Dragons are viewed differently by the characters in this story. Find a different children's book for at least four different characters that represents his or her view of a dragon. Make a poster for the books explaining the selection of each.

Black Ships Before Troy: The Story of the Iliad

20-50-80 Menu

This is a version of the classic story of *The Iliad*. It begins when three of the goddesses fight over an apple that should belong to the most beautiful among them. This argument continues for years until a shepherd named Paris is called upon to settle the argument. Each goddess tries to convince him, but he decides that Aphrodite is in fact the most beautiful. In return, he is promised a beautiful wife. Unfortunately, his new wife already has a husband who is willing to fight in order to have her return home. When the Greeks and Trojans face each other in battle, there can only be one winner.

Reading Objectives Covered Through These Menus and These Activities

- Students will represent textual evidence and use it to prove conclusions.
- Students will compare one literary work with another.
- Students will make and explain inferences made from the story.
- Students will make predictions based on what is read.
- Students will show comprehension by summarizing a story.
- Students will represent textual evidence by using story maps.
- Students will recognize and analyze story plot and problem resolution.

Writing Objectives Covered Through These Menus and These Activities

- Students will write to express their feelings, inform, explain, describe, narrate, entertain, or persuade.
- Students will support their responses with textual evidence.

Materials Needed by Students for Completion

- *Black Ships Before Troy: The Story of the Iliad* by Rosemary Sutcliff
- Microsoft PowerPoint or other slideshow software ■
- Access to other versions of the story of the Iliad
- DVD or VHS recorder (for news reports)
- Story map ▲ ●
- Blank index cards (for trading cards) ▲ ●
- Recycled materials (for models) ▲

Special Notes on the Modifications of These Menus

- If needed, further modifications can be made to a 20-50-80 menu based on the needs of your students. The easiest modification is altering the point goal from 100; lowering or raising the goal on a menu by 10 (or 20) points is appropriate if additional modification up or down is needed.

Special Notes on the Use of These Menus

- These menus give students the opportunity to create a news report. Although students enjoy producing their own videos, there often are difficulties obtaining the equipment and scheduling the use of a video recorder. This activity can be modified by allowing students to act out the product (like a play) or, if students have the technology, allowing them to produce a webcam version of their presentation.
- The triangle menu ▲ asks students to use recycled materials to create their model. This does not mean only plastic and paper; instead, students should focus on using materials in new ways. It works well if a box is started for "recycled" contributions at the beginning of the school year. That way, students always have access to these types of materials.
- The square menu ■ allows students to create a bulletin board display. Some classrooms may only have one bulletin board, so the teacher can divide the board into sections, or additional classroom wall or hall space can be sectioned off for the creation of these displays. Students can plan their display based on the amount of space they are assigned.

Time Frame

- 1–2 weeks—Students are given a menu as the unit is started, and the teacher discusses all of the product options on the menu. As the different options are discussed, students will choose the activities they are most interested in completing so they meet their goal of 100 points. As the lessons progress through the week(s), the teacher and students refer back to the menu options associated with the content being taught.
- 1–2 days—The teacher chooses an activity from the menus to use with the entire class.

Suggested Forms

- All-purpose rubric
- Student presentation rubric
- Proposal form for point-based projects

Black Ships Before Troy

Directions: Choose at least two activities from the options below. The activities must total 100 points. Place a checkmark next to each box to show which activities you will complete. All activities must be completed by: _____.

20 points

❒ Create a model of the horse that was used to trick the Trojans.

❒ Make a drawing of how the Greeks and Trojans dressed for battle.

50 points

❒ Create a set of trading cards for five of the gods and goddesses mentioned in the book.

❒ Complete a story map for *Black Ships Before Troy*.

❒ Create a family tree that shares all of the relationships found in this story.

❒ Design a windowpane that shares at least three examples of symbolism found in this story.

❒ Free choice: Submit a proposal form for a product of your choice.

80 points

❒ Create a news report that shares the events that led up to the Trojan War.

❒ Select another version of *The Iliad* and after reading it, decide which version you feel tells the story better. Design an advertisement for the book you prefer.

Black Ships Before Troy

Directions: Choose at least two activities from the options below. The activities must total 100 points. Place a checkmark next to each box to show which activities you will complete. All activities must be completed by: _____.

---

20 points

❏ Complete a story map for *Black Ships Before Troy*.

❏ Create a set of trading cards for all of the gods and goddesses mentioned in the book.

---

50 points

❏ Design a windowpane that shares at least four examples of symbolism found in this story.

❏ Select another version of *The Iliad* and after reading it, decide which version you feel tells the story better. Design an advertisement for the book you prefer.

❏ Create a family tree that shares all of the relationships found in this story.

❏ Free choice: Submit a proposal form for a product of your choice.

---

80 points

❏ Create a news report that shares the events that led to the Trojan War as well as its proposed resolution.

❏ Perform a play that retells this story from Aphrodite's perspective.

Black Ships Before Troy

Directions: Choose at least two activities from the options below. The activities must total 100 points. Place a checkmark next to each box to show which activities you will complete. All activities must be completed by: _____.

20 points

❑ Design a windowpane that shares at least five examples of symbolism found in this story.

❑ Create a PowerPoint presentation that explains the reason behind the term *Achilles' heel*.

50 points

❑ Select another version of *The Iliad* and after reading it, decide which you feel tells the story better. Design an advertisement for the book you prefer. Your advertisement should share why you believe your selection is the better work.

❑ Perform a play that retells the story of the Trojan Horse from Athena's perceptive.

❑ Luck plays a role in this story. Use a Venn diagram to compare and contrast how luck is used in the story with our present views of it.

❑ Free choice: Submit a proposal form for a product of your choice.

80 points

❑ The Trojan horse has become a famous strategy. Research another event in history that was similar to the Trojan horse. Create a bulletin board display to share your research with your classmates.

❑ Create a news report that shares the events that led to the Trojan War as well as its proposed resolution.

The Diary of Anne Frank: A Play

List Menu

Anne Frank and her family find themselves in a situation where they needed to go into hiding during the reign of the Nazis in World War II. This plays documents their 2-year stay in the secret annex as they try to stay hidden from the Nazis.

Reading Objectives Covered Through These Menus and These Activities

- Students will represent textual evidence and use it to prove conclusions.
- Students will compare one literary work with another.
- Students will interpret figurative language and multiple meaning words.
- Students will make and explain inferences made from the story.
- Students will make predictions based on what is read.
- Students will show comprehension by summarizing a story.
- Students will represent textual evidence by using story maps.
- Students will analyze characters, their relationships, and their importance in the story.
- Students will recognize and analyze story plot and problem resolution.

Writing Objectives Covered Through These Menus and These Activities

- Students will write to express their feelings, inform, explain, describe, and narrate.
- Students will support their responses with textual evidence.
- Students will exhibit voice in their writing.

Materials Needed by Students for Completion

- *The Diary of Anne Frank: A Play* by Frances Goodrich and Albert Hackett
- *Anne Frank: The Diary of a Young Girl* by Anne Frank ● ■
- Poster board or large white paper
- Magazines (for collages)
- Recycled materials (for models)
- Story map ▲
- Internet access (for WebQuests) ● ■
- Microsoft PowerPoint or other slideshow software ● ■
- Scrapbooking materials ▲

Special Notes on the Modifications of These Menus

- Because a List menu is a point-based menu, it is easy to provide additional modifications by simply changing the point goal for those students who need it. The bottom of the menu has a short contract that can be used to record any changes. The two-page format of the triangle and circle menu also allow for additional modification by mixing and matching the pages. The front of each of these two-page menus has the lower and middle-level activities, while the second page has the higher level activities and contract. Additional modifications can be made by using the first page from the circle menu with the second page from the triangle menu. This will allow students a little more flexibility when approaching the higher level activities.

Special Notes on the Use of These Menus

- These menus ask students to use recycled materials to create their models. This does not mean only plastic and paper; instead, students should focus on using materials in new ways. It works well if a box is started for "recycled" contributions at the beginning of the school year. That way, students always have access to these types of materials.
- The circle menu ● allows students to create a bulletin board display. Some classrooms may only have one bulletin board, so the teacher can divide the board into sections, or additional classroom wall or hall space can be sectioned off for the creation of these displays. Students can plan their display based on the amount of space they are assigned.

Time Frame

- 1–2 weeks—Students are given a menu as the unit is started, and the guidelines and point expectations are discussed. Students usually will need to earn 100 points for 100%, although there is an opportunity for extra credit if the teacher would like to use another target number. Because this menu covers one topic in depth, the teacher will go over all of the options for the topic being covered and have students place check marks in the boxes next to the activities they are most interested in completing. Teachers will need to set aside a few moments to sign the agreement at the bottom of the page with each student. As instruction continues, activities are completed by students and submitted to the teacher for grading.
- 1–2 days—The teacher chooses an activity from the menus to use with the entire class.

Suggested Forms

- All-purpose rubric
- Student presentation rubric
- Proposal form for point-based products

Name: _____   ▲

The Diary of Anne Frank: A Play: Side 1

Guidelines:

1. You may complete as many of the activities listed within the time period.
2. You may choose any combination of activities.
3. Your goal is 100 points. You may earn up to _____ points extra credit.
4. You may be as creative as you like within the guidelines listed below.
5. You must show your plan to your teacher by _____.
6. Activities may be turned in at any time during the working time period. They will be graded and recorded on this sheet as you continue to work, so keep it safe!

Plan to Do	Activity to Complete (Side 1: 15–30 points)	Point Value	Date Completed	Points Earned
	Make a model of the diary Anne received for her birthday.	15		
	Complete a story map for this story.	15		
	Design a greeting card that Anne could have given to one of her father's employees who helped during their hiding.	20		
	Create a poster that shares information about the Holocaust.	25		
	Create a model of the building that contained the secret annex.	25		
	Make a timeline that documents Anne's stay in the annex.	25		
	There were things that Anne and her family did without while in the annex. Create a collage of items that would have made their stay easier. Include a sentence about how each would have helped the family.	30		
	Total number of points you are planning to earn from Side 1.	**Total points earned from Side 1:**		

The Diary of Anne Frank: A Play: Side 2

Guidelines:

1. You may complete as many of the activities listed within the time period.
2. You may choose any combination of activities.
3. Your goal is 100 points. You may earn up to _____ points extra credit.
4. You may be as creative as you like within the guidelines listed below.
5. You must show your plan to your teacher by _____.
6. Activities may be turned in at any time during the working time period. They will be graded and recorded on this sheet as you continue to work, so keep it safe!

Plan to Do	Activity to Complete (Side 2: 30–40 points)	Point Value	Date Completed	Points Earned
	Choose an Anne Frank website that you think gives the best information. Share your website with your classmates.	30		
	There are various reasons why people may need to go into hiding. Create a brochure that explains what is needed in hiding and how to not draw attention to you or your family. Base your ideas on the Frank family's experience.	30		
	Turn Anne's diary into a scrapbook of the events that take place.	35		
	What happened to Anne after the play ended? Tell a story to share what happens next.	35		
	Design and keep your own journal for 2 days. (Be sure and give it a meaningful name!) Include daily events and your thoughts about each as they happen.	35		
	Make a list of at least five different emotions Anne experienced during her stay in the Annex. Make a mobile of the emotions with examples of when she experienced each and at least one quote that illustrates the emotion.	35		
	Write a newspaper article about the events that led to the Holocaust and the reasons behind Hitler's actions.	40		
	Free choice: Submit your free choice proposal form for a product of your choice.			
	Total number of points you are planning to earn from Side 1.	**Total points earned from Side 1:**		
	Total number of points you are planning to earn from Side 2.	**Total points earned from Side 2:**		
		Grand Total (/100)		

I am planning to complete _____ activities that could earn up to a total of _____ points.

Teacher's initials _____ Student's signature _____

Name: _____ ●

The Diary of Anne Frank: A Play: Side 1

Guidelines:

1. You may complete as many of the activities listed within the time period.
2. You may choose any combination of activities.
3. Your goal is 100 points. You may earn up to _____ points extra credit.
4. You may be as creative as you like within the guidelines listed below.
5. You must show your plan to your teacher by _____.
6. Activities may be turned in at any time during the working time period. They will be graded and recorded on this sheet as you continue to work, so keep it safe!

Plan to Do	Activity to Complete (Side 1: 10–25 points)	Point Value	Date Completed	Points Earned
	Make a model of the diary Anne received for her birthday.	10		
	Create a poster that shares information about the Holocaust.	15		
	Design a worksheet for your classmates that asks questions about events in this story.	20		
	Write a three facts and a fib about Anne's stay in the annex.	20		
	Create a model of the building that contained the secret annex.	25		
	Make a three-dimensional timeline that documents Anne's stay in the annex.	25		
	There were things that Anne and her family did without while in the annex. Create a collage of items that would have made their stay easier. Include a sentence about how each would have helped the family.	25		
	Total number of points you are planning to earn from Side 1.	**Total points earned from Side 1:**		

Name: _____

The Diary of Anne Frank: A Play: Side 2

Guidelines:

1. You may complete as many of the activities listed within the time period.
2. You may choose any combination of activities.
3. Your goal is 100 points. You may earn up to _____ points extra credit.
4. You may be as creative as you like within the guidelines listed below.
5. You must show your plan to your teacher by _____.
6. Activities may be turned in at any time during the working time period. They will be graded and recorded on this sheet as you continue to work, so keep it safe!

Plan to Do	Activity to Complete (Side 2: 30–40 points)	Point Value	Date Completed	Points Earned
	Read *Anne Frank: Diary of a Young Girl* and write a newspaper article to compare and contrast the two works.	30		
	There are various reasons why people may need to go into hiding. Create a brochure that explains what is needed in hiding and how to not draw attention to you or your family. Base your ideas on the Frank family's experience.	30		
	Why is it important for others to read Anne's story? Design a bulletin board display that shares why others should understand the events and circumstances she discusses.	30		
	Design and keep your own journal for a week. (Be sure and give it a meaningful name!) Include daily events and your thoughts about each as they happen.	35		
	Make a list of at least 10 different emotions Anne experienced during her stay in the annex. Make a PowerPoint of the emotions with examples of when she experienced each and at least one quote that illustrates the emotion.	35		
	Write a newspaper article about the events that led to the Holocaust and the reasons behind Hitler's actions.	35		
	Design a WebQuest that takes questors through information about the Holocaust. Please choose sites that are informational in nature and appropriate for all ages.	40		
	Free choice: Submit your free choice proposal form for a product of your choice.			
	Total number of points you are planning to earn from Side 1.	**Total points earned from Side 1:**		
	Total number of points you are planning to earn from Side 2.	**Total points earned from Side 2:**		
		Grand Total (/100)		

I am planning to complete _____ activities that could earn up to a total of _____ points.

Teacher's initials _____ Student's signature _____

Name: _____ ■

The Diary of Anne Frank: A Play

Guidelines:

1. You may complete as many of the activities listed within the time period.
2. You may choose any combination of activities.
3. Your goal is 100 points. You may earn up to _____ points extra credit.
4. You may be as creative as you like within the guidelines listed below.
5. You must show your plan to your teacher by _____.
6. Activities may be turned in at any time during the working time period. They will be graded and recorded on this sheet as you continue to work, so keep it safe!

Plan to Do	Activity to Complete	Point Value	Date Completed	Points Earned
	Design a book cover for *The Diary of Anne Frank*.	15		
	Gather statistics about the Holocaust and create a pie graph that shows your findings.	15		
	Create a worksheet for the story elements found in *The Diary of Anne Frank*.	20		
	There were things that Anne and her family did without while in the annex. Create a collage of items that would have made their stay easier. Include a paragraph about how each would have helped the family.	20		
	Write a three facts and a fib about Anne's stay in the annex.	20		
	Read *Anne Frank: Diary of a Young Girl* and write an editorial newspaper article to compare and contrast the two works.	25		
	If you could write a letter to Anne Frank today, what would you tell her? Compose the letter.	25		
	Create a cross cut model of the building that contained the secret annex.	25		
	Make a three-dimensional timeline that documents Anne's stay in the annex as well as at least two dates before she entered the annex and two dates after she left.	25		
	There are various reasons why people may need to go into hiding. Create a brochure that explains what is needed in hiding and how to not draw attention to you or your family. Base your ideas on the Frank family's experience.	25		
	Design a WebQuest that takes questors through information about the Holocaust. Please choose sites that are informational in nature and appropriate for all ages.	30		
	Make a list of at least 10 different emotions Anne experienced during her stay in the annex. Make a PowerPoint of the emotions with examples of when she experienced each and at least one quote that illustrates the emotion.	30		
	Free choice: Submit your free choice proposal form for a product of your choice.			
	Total number of points you are planning to earn.		**Total points earned:**	

I am planning to complete _____ activities that could earn up to a total of _____ points.

Teacher's initials _____ Student's signature _____

Sorry, Wrong Number

20-50-80 Menu

Mrs. Stevenson is at home waiting for her husband to return from work. He is running late and when she tries to call him, she connects with a wrong number. During the call, she inadvertently overhears a very disturbing conversation. She takes it upon herself to try and let others know about a crime that is going to be committed. Can she convince them in time?

Reading Objectives Covered Through These Menus and These Activities

- Students will represent textual evidence and use it to prove conclusions.
- Students will interpret figurative language and multiple meaning words.
- Students will make and explain inferences made from the story.
- Students will make predictions based on what is read.
- Students will show comprehension by summarizing a story.
- Students will compare different forms of a written work (written versus performed).
- Students will analyze characters, their relationships, and their importance in the story.
- Students will recognize and analyze story plot and problem resolution.

Writing Objectives Covered Through These Menus and These Activities

- Students will write to express their feelings, inform, explain, describe, narrate, and entertain.
- Students will support their responses with textual evidence.
- Students will exhibit voice in their writing.

Materials Needed by Students for Completion

- *Sorry, Wrong Number* by Louise Fletcher
- Radio recording of *Sorry, Wrong Number* (can be found with an Internet search)
- Poster board or large white paper
- DVD or VHS recorder (for videos ▲ ■, news reports ● ■)
- Recycled materials (for dioramas) ▲ ●

Special Notes on the Modifications of These Menus

- If needed, further modifications can be made to a 20-50-80 menu based on the needs of your students. The easiest modification is altering the point goal from 100; lowering or raising the goal on a menu by 10 (or 20) points is appropriate if additional modification up or down is needed.

Special Notes on the Use of These Menus

- The triangle and circle menus ▲ ● ask students to use recycled materials to create their dioramas. This does not mean only plastic and paper; instead, students should focus on using materials in new ways. It works well if a box is started for "recycled" contributions at the beginning of the school year. That way, students always have access to these types of materials.
- These menus give students the opportunity to create videos ▲ ■ and news reports ● ■. Although students enjoy producing their own videos, there often are difficulties obtaining the equipment and scheduling the use of a video recorder. This activity can be modified by allowing students to act out the product (like a play) or, if students have the technology, allowing them to produce a webcam version of their presentation.

Time Frame

- 1–2 weeks—Students are given a menu as the unit is started, and the teacher discusses all of the product options on the menu. As the different options are discussed, students will choose the activities they are most interested in completing so they meet their goal of 100 points. As the lessons progress through the week(s), the teacher and students refer back to the menu options associated with the content being taught.
- 1–2 days—The teacher chooses an activity from the menus to use with the entire class.

Suggested Forms

- All-purpose rubric
- Student presentation rubric
- Proposal form for point-based projects

Sorry, Wrong Number

Directions: Choose at least two activities from the options below. The activities must total 100 points. Place a checkmark next to each box to show which activities you will complete. All activities must be completed by: _____.

20 points

❐ Retell the events that take place in *Sorry, Wrong Number*.

❐ Make a poster that shows the setting of *Sorry, Wrong Number*.

50 points

❐ Design a brochure that shares how to write a drama in play form. Include instructions for dialogue, scene descriptions, and stage direction.

❐ Based on the scene descriptions, make a diorama that shows how this play would look on stage.

❐ Write a letter to Mrs. Stevenson to tell her any important information she should know.

❐ Free choice: Submit a proposal form for a product of your choice.

80 points

❐ Listen to the original radio recording of *Sorry, Wrong Number*. After listening to the broadcast, record a video to compare and the contrast the two works.

❐ If you could change the ending of the play, what would you have happen? Act out a new ending to the play.

Sorry, Wrong Number

Directions: Choose at least two activities from the options below. The activities must total 100 points. Place a checkmark next to each box to show which activities you will complete. All activities must be completed by: _____.

20 points

❏ Research how phone numbers were different when this play was written. Using the same formula, give at least three examples of how the old system could be used to dial present numbers in our community.

❏ Create a folded quiz book to quiz your classmates about the different literary devices found in this play.

50 points

❏ Listen to the original radio recording of *Sorry, Wrong Number*. After listening to the broadcast, write an editorial newspaper article to compare and the contrast the two works.

❏ Design a brochure that shares how to write a drama in play form. Include instructions for dialogue, scene descriptions, and stage direction.

❏ Based on the set and scene descriptions, make a diorama that could represent how this play would look on stage.

❏ Free choice: Submit a proposal form for a product of your choice.

80 points

❏ Record a news report that covers the events in this play. Be creative about who you interview for your report.

❏ Rewrite the play with Mr. Stevenson as the main character and how the events would appear from his point of the view.

Sorry, Wrong Number

Directions: Choose at least two activities from the options below. The activities must total 100 points. Place a checkmark next to each box to show which activities you will complete. All activities must be completed by: _____.

20 points

- ❏ Research how phone numbers were different when this play was written. Using the same formula, give at least three examples of how the old system could be used to dial present numbers in our community.
- ❏ Design a brochure that shares how to write a drama in play form. Include instructions for dialogue, scene descriptions, and stage direction.

50 points

- ❏ This play was also made into a movie. After watching the movie, write an editorial newspaper article to compare and the contrast the two works.
- ❏ Listen to the original radio recording of *Sorry, Wrong Number*. Record a video that shares your thoughts on the benefits and drawbacks of the radio version of the play.
- ❏ Prepare a news report that covers the events in this play. For your report, be sure and interview the various people Mrs. Stevenson spoke with on the phone, getting their impressions of her.
- ❏ Free choice: Submit a proposal form for a product of your choice.

80 points

- ❏ It has been stated the main character of the play is actually a phone, rather than a person. Write your own play in which an inanimate object is the main character.
- ❏ Select an event in the play that could have changed the outcome Mrs. Stevenson experienced. Rewrite the play from that point including the different ending.

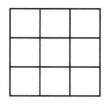

"Blood, Toil, Tears and Sweat"
(Churchill's Address to Parliament on May 13, 1940)

Meal Menu ▲ and Tic-Tac-Toe Menu ● ■

On May 10, 1940, Winston Churchill became Prime Minister of the United Kingdom. Three days after his appointment, he spoke to the House of Commons of the Parliament. His now famous speech centers on his statement that he has "nothing to offer but blood, toil, tears and sweat."

Reading Objectives Covered Through These Menus and These Activities

- Students will represent textual evidence and use it to prove conclusions.
- Students will make and explain inferences made from the story.
- Students will show comprehension by summarizing a speech.
- Students will compare different forms of a written work (written versus performed).

Writing Objectives Covered Through These Menus and These Activities

- Students will write to express their feelings, inform, explain, describe, narrate, entertain, influence, and persuade.
- Students will support their responses with textual evidence.

Materials Needed by Students for Completion

- "Blood, Toil, Tears and Sweat," Winston Churchill's address to Parliament on May 13, 1940 (see p. 132 for a copy of the speech)
- A audio recording of this speech (available online from many websites)
- Poster board or large white paper
- DVD or VHS recorder (for documentaries, news reports) ● ■
- Microsoft PowerPoint or other slideshow software ●
- Map of Europe ▲
- Large lined index cards (for instruction cards) ▲

Special Notes on the Modifications of These Menus

- This topic has two different menu formats: The Meal menu (▲) and Tic-Tac-Toe (● ■) menu. The Meal menu is specifically selected for the triangle option as it easily allows the menu to be broken into manageable bits; the different meals separate the page, making it less daunting for special needs students. The space between the meals makes it easy for the teacher to cut the menu as needed based on the comfort level of the students. If it is the first time choice is being introduced, then the children may receive only the strip of the top breakfast options. Then, when they have finished one of those options, they can receive a strip of lunches and finally the enrichment-level dinner and dessert activities. After students have grown more accustomed to making choices, the menu might be cut just once after the lunch options, so students can select a breakfast and a lunch and submit them to the teacher. Then, they can choose from the dinner strip they receive. The ultimate goal would be for students to have all nine options at once and not be overwhelmed.

Special Notes on the Use of This Menu

- The triangle and square menus ▲ ■ give students the opportunity to create documentaries and news reports. Although students enjoy producing their own videos, there often are difficulties obtaining the equipment and scheduling the use of a video recorder. This activity can be modified by allowing students to act out the product (like a play) or, if students have the technology, allowing them to produce a webcam version of their presentation.
- The triangle and circle menus ▲ ● allow students to create a bulletin board display. Some classrooms may only have one bulletin board, so the teacher can divide the board into sections, or additional classroom wall or hall space can be sectioned off for the creation of these displays. Students can plan their display based on the amount of space they are assigned.

Time Frame

- 2–3 weeks—Students are given a menu as the unit is started. As the teacher presents lessons throughout the week, he or she should refer back to the menu options associated with that content. The teacher will go over all of the options for that content and have students place check marks in the boxes that represent the activities they are most interested in completing. As students choose activities, they should complete a column or a row. When students complete this pattern, they have completed one activity from each content area, learning style, or level of Bloom's revised taxonomy, depending on the design of the menu.

- 1 week—At the start of the unit, the teacher chooses the three activities he or she feels are most valuable for students. Stations can be set up in the classroom. These three activities are available for student choice throughout the week as regular instruction takes place.
- 1–2 days—The teacher chooses an activity from the menus to use with the entire class.

Suggested Forms

- All-purpose rubric
- Student presentation rubric
- Free-choice proposal form

"Blood, Toil, Tears and Sweat"

May 13, 1940
First Speech as Prime Minister to House of Commons

I beg to move,

That this House welcomes the formation of a Government representing the united and inflexible resolve of the nation to prosecute the war with Germany to a victorious conclusion.

On Friday evening last I received His Majesty's commission to form a new Administration. It as the evident wish and will of Parliament and the nation that this should be conceived on the broadest possible basis and that it should include all parties, both those who supported the late Government and also the parties of the Opposition. I have completed the most important part of this task. A War Cabinet has been formed of five Members, representing, with the Opposition Liberals, the unity of the nation. The three party Leaders have agreed to serve, either in the War Cabinet or in high executive office. The three Fighting Services have been filled. It was necessary that this should be done in one single day, on account of the extreme urgency and rigour of events. A number of other positions, key positions, were filled yesterday, and I am submitting a further list to His Majesty to-night. I hope to complete the appointment of the principal Ministers during to-morrow. The appointment of the other Ministers usually takes a little longer, but I trust that, when Parliament meets again, this part of my task will be completed, and that the administration will be complete in all respects.

I considered it in the public interest to suggest that the House should be summoned to meet today. Mr. Speaker agreed, and took the necessary steps, in accordance with the powers conferred upon him by the Resolution of the House. At the end of the proceedings today, the Adjournment of the House will be proposed until Tuesday, 21st May, with, of course, provision for earlier meeting, if need be. The business to be considered during that week will be notified to Members at the earliest opportunity. I now invite the House, by the Motion which stands in my name, to record its approval of the steps taken and to declare its confidence in the new Government.

To form an Administration of this scale and complexity is a serious undertaking in itself, but it must be remembered that we are in the preliminary stage of one of the greatest battles in history, that we are in action at many other points in Norway and in Holland, that we have to be prepared in the Mediterranean, that the air battle is continuous and that many preparations, such as have been indicated by my hon. Friend below the Gangway, have to be made here at home.

In this crisis I hope I may be pardoned if I do not address the House at any length today. I hope that any of my friends and colleagues, or former colleagues, who are affected by the political reconstruction, will make allowance, all allowance, for any lack of ceremony with which it has been necessary to act. I would say to the House, as I said to those who have joined this government: "I have nothing to offer but blood, toil, tears and sweat."

We have before us an ordeal of the most grievous kind. We have before us many, many long months of struggle and of suffering. You ask, what is our policy? I can say: It is to wage war, by sea, land and air, with all our might and with all the strength that God can give us; to wage war against a monstrous tyranny, never surpassed in the dark, lamentable catalogue of human crime. That is our policy. You ask, what is our aim? I can answer in one word: It is victory, victory at all costs, victory in spite of all terror, victory, however long and hard the road may be; for without victory, there is no survival. Let that be realised; no survival for the British Empire, no survival for all that the British Empire has stood for, no survival for the urge and impulse of the ages, that mankind will move forward towards its goal. But I take up my task with buoyancy and hope. I feel sure that our cause will not be suffered to fail among men. At this time I feel entitled to claim the aid of all, and I say, "come then, let us go forward together with our united strength."

"Blood, Toil, Tears and Sweat"

Directions: Choose one activity each for breakfast, lunch, and dinner. Dessert is an activity you can choose to do after you have finished your other meals. All products must be completed by: _____.

Breakfast

❒ On a map of Europe, color all of the places that are mentioned in this speech.

❒ Make a picture dictionary for at least five "new to you" words found in this work.

❒ Make an instruction card that explains how to write a good speech. Use parts of this speech as your example on the card.

Lunch

❒ Make a bulletin board display that shares important information about World War II.

❒ Design a poster that shares information about Winston Churchill before he became the Prime Minister.

❒ Create a timeline for the events that led up to this speech.

Dinner

❒ Listen to a recording of Churchill giving this speech. Create a Venn diagram comparing reading the speech to simply listening to it.

❒ Make a mind map that shares the ideas Churchill used in his speech.

❒ Free choice: Submit a free choice proposal about this speech to your teacher for approval.

Dessert

❒ Revisit Churchill's speech and rewrite it in a way that makes it easier for others to understand.

❒ Come to school as Winston Churchill and share one part of his speech with your classmates.

Name: _____

"Blood, Toil, Tears and Sweat"

Directions: Check the boxes you plan to complete. They should form a tic-tac-toe across or down. All products are due by: _____.

☐ The History	☐ The Content	☐ The Evaluation
Perform a news report that shares the world events that led up to "Blood, Toil, Tears and Sweat."	Make a mind map that addresses the topics, details, and specific words and phrases Churchill used in his speech.	Listen to a recording of Churchill giving this speech. Create a Venn diagram comparing and contrasting the impact of reading the speech to simply listening to it.
☐ The Evaluation	☐ **Free Choice:** *On the history behind this speech* (Fill out your proposal form before beginning the free choice!)	☐ The Content
This is considered one of the greatest speeches in history. Research why historians believe this to be true. Create a PowerPoint presentation sharing your research. Refer to at least two sources.		Record a video documentary that discusses the way phrases and ideas were shared in Churchill's speech.
☐ The Content	☐ The Evaluation	☐ The History
Revisit Churchill's speech and rewrite it in terms and ideas that may be easier for others to understand.	Select the most persuasive part of this speech. Come to school as Winston Churchill and share the part you have selected.	Make a bulletin board display that shares important information about World War II.

Name: _____ ■

"Blood, Toil, Tears and Sweat"

Directions: Check the boxes you plan to complete. They should form a tic-tac-toe across or down. All products are due by: _____.

☐ **The History**	☐ **The Content**	☐ **The Evaluation**
Perform a news report that shares the events that led up to "Blood, Toil, Tears and Sweat." Focus on the events that are referenced in Churchill's speech.	Select a quote from the speech (other than its title) that you think is persuasive. Make a poster for this quote explaining its importance to the speech and why you selected it.	Listen to a recording of Churchill giving this speech. Create a brochure that shares information on making a powerful speech. Include whether hearing or reading a speech has a greater impact on the audience.
☐ **The Evaluation**	☐ **Free Choice:** *On the history behind this speech* (Fill out your proposal form before beginning the free choice!)	☐ **The Content**
Is Churchill the first to use these four words together to convey a message? Research the background behind his speech to determine its originality. Write an essay to share your findings.		Record a video documentary that discusses Churchill's specific use of words and vocabulary in his speech. Your documentary should include at least two interviews with people who heard the speech, asking their opinion about its context.
☐ **The Content**	☐ **The Evaluation**	☐ **The History**
Revisit Churchill's speech and translate it into terms and ideas that may be easier for others to understand. Your translation may need to be longer than the speech, as you may need to provide background information to make the information clearer.	This speech is considered one of the greatest speeches ever given. Write and give your own speech defending or opposing this view. Be sure to include quotes from his speech to prove your point.	Not everyone believed that Churchill was the right man for the Prime Minister position. Write a letter that someone who opposed his appointment may have sent, detailing his or her reasons why another person would have been a better choice.

CHAPTER 6

Poetry

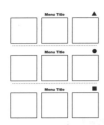

"Paul Revere's Ride"

Poetry Shape Menu

Reading Objectives Covered Through This Menu and These Activities

- Students will interpret figurative language and multiple meaning words.
- Students will make predictions based on what is read.
- Students will use resources and references to build meaning.

Writing Objectives Covered Through This Menu and These Activities

- Students will write to express their feelings, reflect, inform, explain, describe, or narrate.
- Students will use vivid language.
- Students will exhibit voice in their writing.

Materials Needed by Students for Completion

- "Paul Revere's Ride" by Henry Wadsworth Longfellow (p. 140)
- Other narrative poems written by Henry Wadsworth Longfellow
- Map of New England ▲
- Story map ▲
- Recycled materials (for dioramas) ▲
- DVD or VHS recorder (for videos) ●

Special Notes on the Modifications of This Menu

- This menu is unique from the others, as teachers can select the number of choices based on the amount of time they plan to spend processing a particular poem. This menu is divided into three sections, the top ▲ or triangle section has activities with the most modifications, the middle ● or circle section has activities with minor modifications, and the lower ■ or square section has activities that offer the most extension. If the goal is to have students create one product for the poem, then the teacher can provide each student with a strip of an appropriate level of options. For a more in-depth study, the teacher can provide the entire menu and students select one option from each section of the menu.

Special Notes on the Use of This Menu

- The circle menu ● gives students the opportunity to create a video. Although students enjoy producing their own videos, there often are difficulties obtaining the equipment and scheduling the use of a video recorder. This activity can be modified by allowing students to act out the product (like a play) or, if students have the technology, allowing them to produce a webcam version of their product.
- The triangle menu ▲ asks students to use recycled materials to create their diorama. This does not mean only plastic and paper; instead, students should focus on using materials in new ways. It works well if a box is started for "recycled" contributions at the beginning of the school year. That way, students always have access to these types of materials.

Time Frame

- 1 week—Students are given the menu before the poem is read. The teacher will go over all of the options for the menu and have students indicate each option that represents the activity they are most interested in completing. The teacher may assign the menu as independent work or choose to allow students time to work after their other work is finished.
- 1–2 days—The teacher chooses a strip for each student to complete based on his or her specific needs. The student selects one of the activities on the strip and works on it for independent practice.

Suggested Forms

- All-purpose rubric
- Student presentation rubric

Paul Revere's Ride

by Henry Wadsworth Longfellow

Listen, my children, and you shall hear
Of the midnight ride of Paul Revere,
On the eighteenth of April, in Seventy-five;
Hardly a man is now alive
Who remembers that famous day and year.

He said to his friend, "If the British march
By land or sea from the town to-night,
Hang a lantern aloft in the belfry arch
Of the North Church tower as a signal light,—
One, if by land, and two, if by sea;
And I on the opposite shore will be,
Ready to ride and spread the alarm
Through every Middlesex village and farm
For the country folk to be up and to arm,"

Then he said, "Good night!" and with muffled oar
Silently rowed to the Charlestown shore,
Just as the moon rose over the bay,
Where swinging wide at her moorings lay
The Somerset, British man-of-war;
A phantom ship, with each mast and spar
Across the moon like a prison bar,
And a huge black hulk, that was magnified
By its own reflection in the tide.

Meanwhile, his friend, through alley and street,
Wanders and watches with eager ears,
Till in the silence around him he hears
The muster of men at the barrack door,
The sound of arms, and the tramp of feet,
And the measured tread of the grenadiers,
Marching down to their boats on the shore.

Then he climbed the tower of the Old North Church,
By the wooden stairs, with stealthy tread,
To the belfry-chamber overhead,

And startled the pigeons from their perch
On the sombre rafters, that round him made
Masses and moving shapes of shade,—
By the trembling ladder, steep and tall
To the highest window in the wall,
Where he paused to listen and look down
A moment on the roofs of the town,
And the moonlight flowing over all.

Beneath, in the churchyard, lay the dead,
In their night-encampment on the hill,
Wrapped in silence so deep and still
That he could hear, like a sentinel's tread,
The watchful night-wind, as it went
Creeping along from tent to tent
And seeming to whisper, "All is well!"
A moment only he feels the spell
Of the place and the hour, and the secret dread
Of the lonely belfry and the dead;
For suddenly all his thoughts are bent
On a shadowy something far away,
Where the river widens to meet the bay,—
A line of black that bends and floats
On the rising tide, like a bridge of boats.

Meanwhile, impatient to mount and ride,
Booted and spurred, with a heavy stride
On the opposite shore walked Paul Revere.
Now he patted his horse's side,
Now gazed at the landscape far and near,
Then, impetuous, stamped the earth,
And turned and tightened his saddle-girth;
But mostly he watched with eager search
The belfry-tower of the Old North Church,
As it rose above the graves on the hill,
Lonely and spectral and sombre and still.
And lo! as he looks, on the belfry's height
A glimmer, and then a gleam of light!
He springs to the saddle, the bridle he turns,
But lingers and gazes, till full on his sight
A second lamp in the belfry burns!

A hurry of hoofs in a village street,
A shape in the moonlight, a bulk in the dark,
And beneath, from the pebbles, in passing, a spark
Struck out by a steed flying fearless and fleet:
That was all! And yet, through the gloom and the light,
The fate of a nation was riding that night;
And the spark struck out by that steed, in his flight,
Kindled the land into flame with its heat.
He has left the village and mounted the steep,
And beneath him, tranquil and broad and deep,
Is the Mystic, meeting the ocean tides;
And under the alders, that skirt its edge,
Now soft on the sand, now loud on the ledge,
Is heard the tramp of his steed as he rides.

It was twelve by the village clock
When he crossed the bridge into Medford town.
He heard the crowing of the cock,
And the barking of the farmer's dog,
And felt the damp of the river fog,
That rises after the sun goes down.

It was one by the village clock,
When he galloped into Lexington.
He saw the gilded weathercock
Swim in the moonlight as he passed,
And the meeting-house windows, blank and bare,
Gaze at him with a spectral glare,
As if they already stood aghast
At the bloody work they would look upon.

It was two by the village clock,
When he came to the bridge in Concord town.
He heard the bleating of the flock,
And the twitter of birds among the trees,
And felt the breath of the morning breeze
Blowing over the meadows brown.
And one was safe and asleep in his bed
Who at the bridge would be first to fall,
Who that day would be lying dead,
Pierced by a British musket-ball.

You know the rest. In the books you have read,
How the British Regulars fired and fled,—
How the farmers gave them ball for ball,
From behind each fence and farm-yard wall,
Chasing the red-coats down the lane,
Then crossing the fields to emerge again
Under the trees at the turn of the road,
And only pausing to fire and load.

So through the night rode Paul Revere;
And so through the night went his cry of alarm
To every Middlesex village and farm,—
A cry of defiance and not of fear,
A voice in the darkness, a knock at the door,
And a word that shall echo forevermore!
For, borne on the night-wind of the Past,
Through all our history, to the last,
In the hour of darkness and peril and need,
The people will waken and listen to hear
The hurrying hoof-beats of that steed,
And the midnight message of Paul Revere.

"Paul Revere's Ride"

Directions: Select one of the following options.

On a map of New England, label all of the locations the poem shares and mark the route that Paul Revere took on his ride.

Complete a story map for "Paul Revere's Ride."

Make a diorama of the most important scene in "Paul Revere's Ride."

"Paul Revere's Ride"

Directions: Select one of the following options.

Consider if Paul Revere's ride had failed. Write a story to share the events that may have followed and its impact on history.

Compare and contrast the information provided in the poem with historical accounts of the event. Record a video to share what is factual and what is not.

Make a three-dimensional timeline that shares the events that led up to and including Paul Revere's ride.

"Paul Revere's Ride"

Directions: Select one of the following options.

Write and perform a song that tells the story of another historical event that followed the ride discussed in this poem.

Select another narrative poem by Henry Wadsworth Longfellow. Write an essay to compare and contrast the literary elements found in each.

Write a narrative poem about another historical event using the same rhyme scheme that "Paul Revere's Ride" uses.

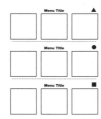

"O Captain! My Captain!"

Poetry Shape Menu

Reading Objectives Covered Through This Menu and These Activities

- Students will compare one literary work with another.
- Students will interpret figurative language and multiple meaning words.
- Students will make predictions based on what is read.
- Students will use resources and references to build meaning.

Writing Objectives Covered Through This Menu and These Activities

- Students will write to express their feelings, reflect, inform, explain, describe, or narrate.
- Students will use vivid language.
- Students will exhibit voice in their writing.

Materials Needed by Students for Completion

- "O Captain! My Captain!" by Walt Whitman (p. 147)
- DVD or VHS recorder or voice recorder ▲
- Poster board or large white paper

Special Notes on the Modifications of This Menu

- This menu is unique from the others, as teachers can select the number of choices based on the amount of time they plan to spend processing a particular poem. This menu is divided into three sections, the top ▲ or triangle section has activities with the most modifications, the middle ● or circle section has activities with minor modifications, and the lower ■ or square section has activities that offer the most extension. If the goal is to have students create one product for the poem, then the teacher can provide each student with a strip of an appropriate level of options. For a more in-depth study, the teacher can provide the entire menu and students select one option from each section of the menu.

Special Notes on the Use of This Menu

- The triangle menu ▲ gives students the opportunity to create a video or voice recording. Although students enjoy producing their own recordings, there often are difficulties obtaining the equipment and scheduling the use of a recorder. This activity can be modified by allowing students to act out the product (like a play) or, if students have the technology, allowing them to produce a webcam version of their product.

Time Frame

- 1 week—Students are given the menu before the poem is read. The teacher will go over all of the options for the menu and have students indicate each option that represents the activity they are most interested in completing. The teacher may assign the menu as independent work or choose to allow students time to work after their other work is finished.
- 1–2 days—The teacher chooses a strip for each student to complete based on his or her specific needs. The student selects one of the activities on the strip and works on it for independent practice.

Suggested Forms

- All-purpose rubric
- Student presentation rubric
- Student-taught lesson rubric

O Captain! My Captain!

by Walt Whitman

O Captain! my Captain! our fearful trip is done;
The ship has weather'd every rack, the prize we sought is won;
The port is near, the bells I hear, the people all exulting,
While follow eyes the steady keel, the vessel grim and daring:
But O heart! heart! heart!
O the bleeding drops of red,
Where on the deck my Captain lies,
Fallen cold and dead.

O Captain! my Captain! rise up and hear the bells;
Rise up—for you the flag is flung—for you the bugle trills;
For you bouquets and ribbon'd wreaths—for you the shores a-crowding;
For you they call, the swaying mass, their eager faces turning;
Here Captain! dear father!
This arm beneath your head;
It is some dream that on the deck,
You've fallen cold and dead.

My Captain does not answer, his lips are pale and still;
My father does not feel my arm, he has no pulse nor will;
The ship is anchor'd safe and sound, its voyage closed and done;
From fearful trip, the victor ship, comes in with object won;
Exult, O shores, and ring, O bells!
But I, with mournful tread,
Walk the deck my Captain lies,
Fallen cold and dead.

"O Captain! My Captain!"

Directions: Select one of the following options.   ▲

Write a summary of what happens in the poem.	Record yourself doing a dramatic reading of "O Captain! My Captain!"	Make a drawing of the scene described in this poem.

"O Captain! My Captain!"

Directions: Select one of the following options.   ●

Make a flipbook with pairs of all of the metaphors found in this poem, with their meanings.	Find another poem about this event. Make a poster to compare the two works and how they tell the story.	Make "O Captain! My Captain!" into a children's book with school-appropriate illustrations.

"O Captain! My Captain!"

Directions: Select one of the following options.   ■

Perform a speech that conveys the same emotion about the event described in "O Captain! My Captain!"	Prepare a written student-taught lesson in which you further analyze this poem.	Select an important historical event and write a poem in the style of "O Captain! My Captain!" Focus on the poems structure and use of metaphors.

"Jabberwocky"

Poetry Shape Menu

Reading Objectives Covered Through This Menu and These Activities

- Students will interpret figurative language and multiple meaning words.
- Students will make predictions based on what is read.
- Students will use resources and references to build meaning.

Writing Objectives Covered Through This Menu and These Activities

- Students will write to express their feelings, reflect, inform, explain, describe, or narrate.
- Students will use vivid language.
- Students will exhibit voice in their writing.

Materials Needed by Students for Completion

- "Jabberwocky" by Lewis Carroll (p. 151)
- Blank index cards (for trading cards ■, concentration cards ▲)
- Ruler (for comic strips) ●
- Poster board or large white paper
- DVD or VHS recorder (for dramatic production) ■

Special Notes on the Modifications of This Menu

- This menu is unique from the others, as teachers can select the number of choices based on the amount of time they plan to spend processing a particular poem. This menu is divided into three sections, the top ▲ or triangle section has activities with the most modifications, the middle ● or circle section has activities with minor modifications, and the lower ■ or square section has activities that offer the most extension. If the goal is to have students create one product for the poem, then the teacher can provide each student with a strip of an appropriate level of options. For a more in-depth study, the teacher can provide the entire menu and students select one option from each section of the menu.

Special Notes on the Use of This Menu

- The square strip of this menu ■ gives students the opportunity to create a dramatic production with the option of recording it as a video. Although students enjoy producing their own videos, there often are difficulties obtaining the equipment and scheduling the use of a video recorder. This activity can be modified by allowing students to act out the product (like a play) or, if students have the technology, allowing them to produce a webcam version of their product.

Time Frame

- 1 week—Students are given the menu before the poem is read. The teacher will go over all of the options for the menu and have students indicate each option that represents the activity they are most interested in completing. The teacher may assign the menu as independent work or choose to allow students time to work after their other work is finished.
- 1–2 days—The teacher chooses a strip for each student to complete based on his or her specific needs. The student selects one of the activities on the strip and works on it for independent practice.

Suggested Forms

- All-purpose rubric
- Student presentation rubric

Jabberwocky

by Lewis Carroll

'Twas brillig, and the slithy toves
Did gyre and gimble in the wabe:
All mimsy were the borogoves,
And the mome raths outgrabe.

"Beware the Jabberwock, my son!
The jaws that bite, the claws that catch!
Beware the Jubjub bird, and shun
The frumious Bandersnatch!"

He took his vorpal sword in hand:
Long time the manxome foe he sought,
So rested he by the Tumtum tree,
And stood a while in thought.

And, as in uffish thought he stood,
The Jabberwock, with eyes of flame,
Came whiffling through the tulgey wood,
And burbled as it came!

One two! One two! And through and through
The vorpal blade went snicker-snack!
He left it dead, and with its head
He went galumphing back.

"And hast thou slain the Jabberwock?
Come to my arms, my beamish boy!
Oh frabjous day! Callooh! Callay!"
He chortled in his joy.

'Twas brillig, and the slithy toves
Did gyre and gimble in the wabe:
All mimsy were the borogoves,
And the mome raths outgrabe.

Name: _____

"Jabberwocky"

Directions: Select one of the following options. ▲

Make a drawing to represent what happens in Jabberwocky.

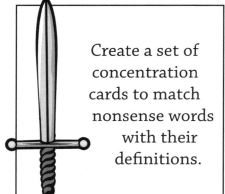
Create a set of concentration cards to match nonsense words with their definitions.

Rewrite Jabberwocky in everyday terms.

- -

"Jabberwocky"

Directions: Select one of the following options. ●

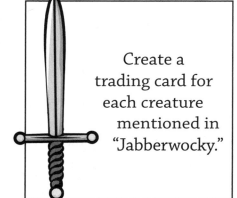
Create a trading card for each creature mentioned in "Jabberwocky."

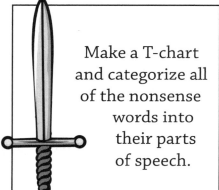
Make a T-chart and categorize all of the nonsense words into their parts of speech.

Make a comic strip featuring one of the creatures in Jabberwocky.

- -

"Jabberwocky"

Directions: Select one of the following options. ■

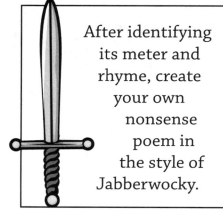
After identifying its meter and rhyme, create your own nonsense poem in the style of Jabberwocky.

Consider how Lewis Carroll developed the words he used in this poem. Create your own picture dictionary with at least 15 nonsense words that could sound reasonable.

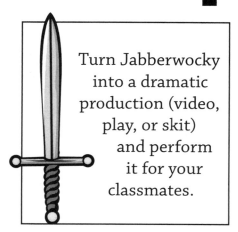
Turn Jabberwocky into a dramatic production (video, play, or skit) and perform it for your classmates.

"The Railway Train"

Poetry Shape Menu

Reading Objectives Covered Through This Menu and These Activities

- Students will interpret figurative language and multiple meaning words.
- Students will make predictions based on what is read.
- Students will use resources and references to build meaning.

Writing Objectives Covered Through This Menu and These Activities

- Students will write to express their feelings, reflect, inform, explain, describe, or narrate.
- Students will use vivid language.
- Students will exhibit voice in their writing.

Materials Needed by Students for Completion

- "The Railway Train" by Emily Dickinson (p. 155)
- Recycled materials (for dioramas) ▲
- Microsoft PowerPoint or other slideshow software ■

Special Notes on the Modifications of This Menu

- This menu is unique from the others, as teachers can select the number of choices based on the amount of time they plan to spend processing a particular poem. This menu is divided into three sections, the top ▲ or triangle section has activities with the most modifications, the middle ● or circle section has activities with minor modifications, and the lower ■ or square section has activities that offer the most extension. If the goal is to have students create one product for the poem, then the teacher can provide each student with a strip of an appropriate level of options. For a more in-depth study, the teacher can provide the entire menu and students select one option from each section of the menu.

Special Notes on the Use of This Menu

- The circle menu ● asks students to use recycled materials to create their dioramas. This does not mean only plastic and paper; instead, students should focus on using materials in new ways. It works well if a box is started for "recycled" contributions at the beginning of the school year. That way, students always have access to these types of materials.

Time Frame

- 1 week—Students are given the menu before the poem is read. The teacher will go over all of the options for the menu and have students indicate each option that represents the activity they are most interested in completing. The teacher may assign the menu as independent work or choose to allow students time to work after their other work is finished.
- 1–2 days—The teacher chooses a strip for each student to complete based on his or her specific needs. The student selects one of the activities on the strip and works on it for independent practice.

Suggested Forms

- All-purpose rubric
- Student presentation rubric
- Student-taught lesson rubric

The Railway Train

by Emily Dickinson

I like to see it lap the miles,
And lick the valleys up,
And stop to feed itself at tanks;
And then, prodigious, step

Around a pile of mountains,
And, supercilious, peer
In shanties, by the sides of roads;
And then a quarry pare

To fit its sides, and crawl between,
Complaining all the while
In horrid, hooting stanza;
Then chase itself down hill

And neigh like Boanerges;
Then, punctual as a star,
Stop—docile and omnipotent—
At its own stable door.

"The Railway Train"

Directions: Select one of the following options. ▲

Make a drawing or illustration for "The Railway Train."	Design an acrostic for the title of this poem. Use words to describe the train for each letter.	Create a diorama that shows one of the activities the train does in this poem.

- -

"The Railway Train"

Directions: Select one of the following options. ●

Use a Venn diagram to compare the train with the animal described in the poem.	Write a three facts and a fib about the train and its comparison to a living thing.	Perform a dramatic reading of "The Railway Train." Your reading should include sound effects and appropriate hand motions.

- -

"The Railway Train"

Directions: Select one of the following options. ■

Write your own poem in which you compare an object to an animal.	Prepare a PowerPoint presentation that shows how this poem is historically significant to the period in which it was written.	Prepare a student-taught lesson on the analysis of "The Railway Train."

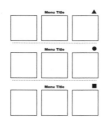

"The Song of Wandering Aengus"

Poetry Shape Menu

Reading Objectives Covered Through This Menu and These Activities

- Students will interpret figurative language and multiple meaning words.
- Students will make predictions based on what is read.
- Students will use resources and references to build meaning.

Writing Objectives Covered Through This Menu and These Activities

- Students will write to express their feelings, reflect, inform, explain, describe, or narrate.
- Students will use vivid language.
- Students will exhibit voice in their writing.

Materials Needed by Students for Completion

- "The Song of Wandering Aengus" by William Butler Yeats (p. 159)
- Poster board or large white paper
- Magazines (for collages) ▲
- DVD or VHS recorder (for videos) ■

Special Notes on the Modifications of This Menu

- This menu is unique from the others, as teachers can select the number of choices based on the amount of time they plan to spend processing a particular poem. This menu is divided into three sections, the top ▲ or triangle section has activities with the most modifications, the middle ● or circle section has activities with minor modifications, and the lower ■ or square section has activities that offer the most extension. If the goal is to have students create one product for the poem, then the teacher can provide each student with a strip of an appropriate level of options. For a more in-depth study, the teacher can provide the entire menu and students select one option from each section of the menu.

Special Notes on the Use of This Menu

- The square strip of this menu ■ gives students the opportunity to create a video. Although students enjoy producing their own videos, there often are difficulties obtaining the equipment and scheduling the use of a video recorder. This activity can be modified by allowing students to act out the product (like a play) or, if students have the technology, allowing them to produce a webcam version of their product.

Time Frame

- 1 week—Students are given the menu before the poem is read. The teacher will go over all of the options for the menu and have students indicate each option that represents the activity they are most interested in completing. The teacher may assign the menu as independent work or choose to allow students time to work after their other work is finished.
- 1–2 days—The teacher chooses a strip for each student to complete based on his or her specific needs. The student selects one of the activities on the strip and works on it for independent practice.

Suggested Forms

- All-purpose rubric
- Student presentation rubric

The Song of Wandering Aengus
by William Butler Yeats

I went out to the hazel wood,
Because a fire was in my head,
And cut and peeled a hazel wand,
And hooked a berry to a thread;
And when white moths were on the wing,
And moth-like stars were flickering out,
I dropped the berry in a stream
And caught a little silver trout.

When I had laid it on the floor
I went to blow the fire a-flame,
But something rustled on the floor,
And someone called me by my name:
It had become a glimmering girl
With apple blossom in her hair
Who called me by my name and ran
And faded through the brightening air.

Though I am old with wandering
Through hollow lands and hilly lands,
I will find out where she has gone,
And kiss her lips and take her hands;
And walk among long dappled grass,
And pluck till time and times are done,
The silver apples of the moon,
The golden apples of the sun.

"The Song of Wandering Aengus"

Directions: Select one of the following options.

Write a worksheet for "The Song of Wandering Aengus."

Create a poster that shares information about the Irish god, Aengus.

Make a collage of the words that are most commonly repeated in this poem.

- -

"The Song of Wandering Aengus"

Directions: Select one of the following options.

Create a children's book for "The Song of Wandering Aengus," however, you have to tell the story of the poem without using any words.

Make a windowpane in which you provide examples of at least five different literary devices found in this poem.

Write a three facts and a fib about the writing style used in "The Song of Wandering Aengus."

- -

"The Song of Wandering Aengus"

Directions: Select one of the following options.

Record a video that shares the poem's message and how it relates to your life.

Prepare a presentation of an original musical song that has the same tone and style as "The Song of Wandering Aengus."

Consider the message of this poem and write your own modern poem with a similar message and style.

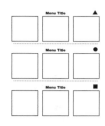

"The Road Not Taken"

Poetry Shape Menu

Reading Objectives Covered Through This Menu and These Activities

- Students will compare one literary work with another.
- Students will interpret figurative language and multiple meaning words.
- Students will make predictions based on what is read.
- Students will use resources and references to build meaning.

Writing Objectives Covered Through This Menu and These Activities

- Students will write to express their feelings, reflect, inform, explain, describe, or narrate.
- Students will use vivid language.
- Students will exhibit voice in their writing.

Materials Needed by Students for Completion

- "The Road Not Taken" by Robert Frost
- Other poems by Robert Frost
- Voice recorder ▲ or DVD or VHS recorder (for videos) ▲ ■
- Poster board or large white paper
- Magazines (for collages) ●
- Literary Analysis Cube template ●

Special Notes on the Modifications of This Menu

- This menu is unique from the others, as teachers can select the number of choices based on the amount of time they plan to spend processing a particular poem. This menu is divided into three sections, the top ▲ or triangle section has activities with the most modifications, the middle ● or circle section has activities with minor modifications, and the lower ■ or square section has activities that offer the most extension. If the goal is to have students create one product for the poem, then the teacher can provide each student with a strip of an appropriate level of options. For a more in-depth study, the teacher can provide the entire menu and students select one option from each section of the menu.

Special Notes on the Use of This Menu

- The triangle and square strips of the menu ▲ ■ give students the opportunity to create a video. Although students enjoy producing their own videos, there often are difficulties obtaining the equipment and scheduling the use of a video recorder. This activity can be modified by allowing students to act out the product (like a play) or, if students have the technology, allowing them to produce a webcam version of their product.

Time Frame

- 1 week—Students are given the menu before the poem is read. The teacher will go over all of the options for the menu and have students indicate each option that represents the activity they are most interested in completing. The teacher may assign the menu as independent work or choose to allow students time to work after their other work is finished.
- 1–2 days—The teacher chooses a strip for each student to complete based on his or her specific needs. The student selects one of the activities on the strip and works on it for independent practice.

Suggested Forms

- All-purpose rubric
- Student presentation rubric

The Road Not Taken

by Robert Frost

Two roads diverged in a yellow wood,
And sorry I could not travel both
And be one traveler, long I stood
And looked down one as far as I could
To where it bent in the undergrowth;

Then took the other, as just as fair
And having perhaps the better claim,
Because it was grassy and wanted wear;
Though as for that, the passing there
Had worn them really about the same,

And both that morning equally lay
In leaves no step had trodden black
Oh, I kept the first for another day!
Yet knowing how way leads on to way,
I doubted if I should ever come back.

I shall be telling this with a sigh
Somewhere ages and ages hence:
Two roads diverged in a wood, and I,
I took the one less traveled by,
And that has made all the difference.

Name: _____

"The Road Not Taken"

Directions: Select one of the following options.   ▲

Create an illustration for this poem to show all of the details the writer describes.

Record yourself reading this poem for your classmates.

Make a poster to share information about Robert Frost and his works.

- -

"The Road Not Taken"

Directions: Select one of the following options.   ●

Make a collage of photos that could be used to represent the meaning of this poem. Label each photo with a sentence explaining how it is related.

Select another poem by Robert Frost and use a Venn diagram to compare the style of both poems.

Complete "The Road Not Taken" Literary Analysis Cube.

- -

"The Road Not Taken"

Directions: Select one of the following options.   ■

Pretend you are 30 years old. Write a story in which you look back on your life since middle school and share a story in which you took the road less traveled.

Create a video in which you promote or discourage the audience to make the same decision Robert Frost made in "The Road Not Taken."

Write an original poem that shares what happens when someone chooses the path that Robert Frost selected in the poem.

"The Road Not Taken" Literary Analysis Cube   ●

Provide an example from "The Road Not Taken" for each literary device. Place your example on each side of the cube. Include a quote if needed.

Use this pattern or create your own cube. You may choose to put questions or statements on each side of your cube.

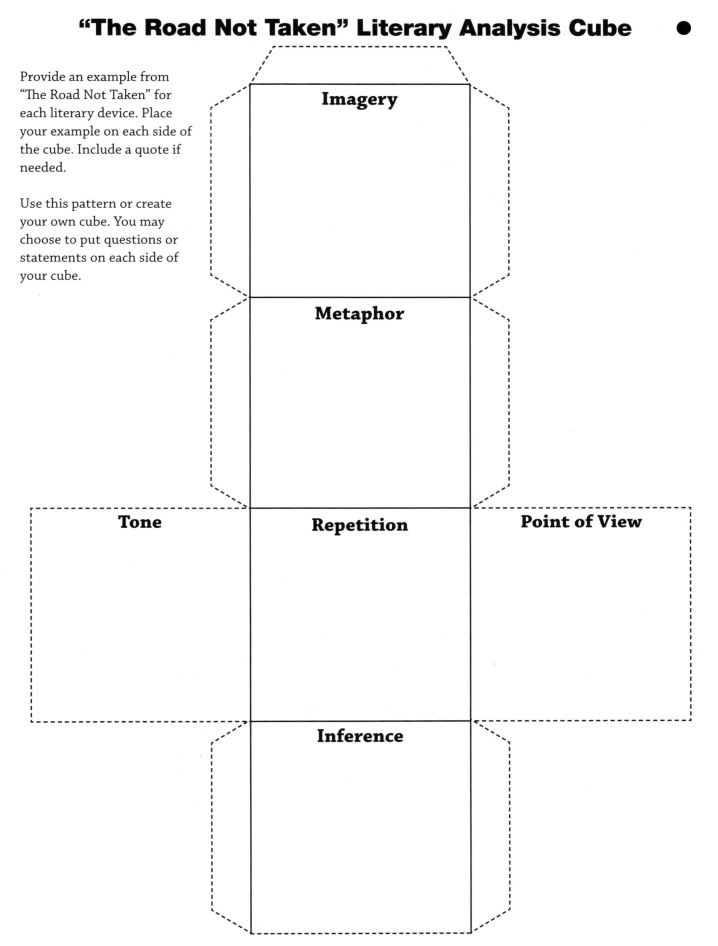

Imagery

Metaphor

Tone   **Repetition**   **Point of View**

Inference

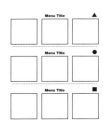

"Chicago"

Poetry Shape Menu

Reading Objectives Covered Through This Menu and These Activities

- Students will compare one literary work with another.
- Students will interpret figurative language and multiple meaning words.
- Students will make predictions based on what is read.
- Students will use resources and references to build meaning.

Writing Objectives Covered Through This Menu and These Activities

- Students will write to express their feelings, reflect, inform, explain, describe, or narrate.
- Students will use vivid language.
- Students will exhibit voice in their writing.

Materials Needed by Students for Completion

- "Chicago" by Carl Sandburg (p. 168–169)
- Other poems by Carl Sandburg
- Magazines or Internet images (for collages) ▲
- Poster board or large white paper
- Blank index cards (for concentration cards) ▲
- Microsoft PowerPoint or other slideshow software ■
- DVD or VHS recorder (for commercials) ■

Special Notes on the Modifications of This Menu

- This menu is unique from the others, as teachers can select the number of choices based on the amount of time they plan to spend processing a particular poem. This menu is divided into three sections, the top ▲ or triangle section has activities with the most modifications, the middle ● or circle section has activities with minor modifications, and the lower ■ or square section has activities that offer the most extension. If the goal is to have students create one product for the poem, then the teacher can provide each student with a strip of an appropriate level of options. For a more in-depth study, the teacher can provide the entire menu and students select one option from each section of the menu.

Special Notes on the Use of This Menu

- The square strip of the menu ■ gives students the opportunity to create a video. Although students enjoy producing their own videos, there often are difficulties obtaining the equipment and scheduling the use of a video recorder. This activity can be modified by allowing students to act out the product (like a play) or, if students have the technology, allowing them to produce a webcam version of their product.

Time Frame

- 1 week—Students are given the menu before the poem is read. The teacher will go over all of the options for the menu and have students indicate each option that represents the activity they are most interested in completing. The teacher may assign the menu as independent work or choose to allow students time to work after their other work is finished.
- 1–2 days—The teacher chooses a strip for each student to complete based on his or her specific needs. The student selects one of the activities on the strip and works on it for independent practice.

Suggested Forms

- All-purpose rubric
- Student presentation rubric

Chicago

by Carl Sandburg

Hog Butcher for the World,
   Tool Maker, Stacker of Wheat,
   Player with Railroads and the Nation's Freight Handler;
   Stormy, husky, brawling,
   City of the Big Shoulders:

They tell me you are wicked and I believe them, for I
   have seen your painted women under the gas lamps
   luring the farm boys.
And they tell me you are crooked and I answer: Yes, it
   is true I have seen the gunman kill and go free to
   kill again.
And they tell me you are brutal and my reply is: On the
   faces of women and children I have seen the marks
   of wanton hunger.
And having answered so I turn once more to those who
   sneer at this my city, and I give them back the sneer
   and say to them:
Come and show me another city with lifted head singing
   so proud to be alive and coarse and strong and cunning.
Flinging magnetic curses amid the toil of piling job on
   job, here is a tall bold slugger set vivid against the
   little soft cities;

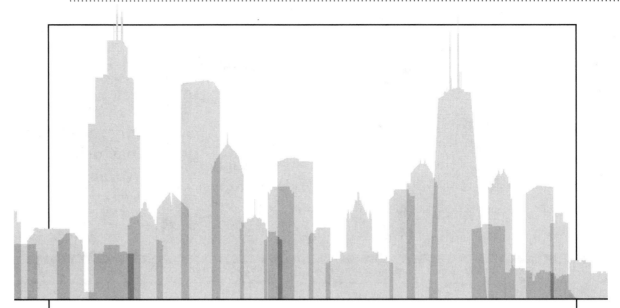

Fierce as a dog with tongue lapping for action, cunning
  as a savage pitted against the wilderness,
    Bareheaded,
    Shoveling,
    Wrecking,
    Planning,
    Building, breaking, rebuilding,
Under the smoke, dust all over his mouth, laughing
  with white teeth,
Under the terrible burden of destiny laughing as a young
   man laughs,
Laughing even as an ignorant fighter laughs who has
  never lost a battle,
Bragging and laughing that under his wrist is the pulse.
  and under his ribs the heart of the people,
     Laughing!
Laughing the stormy, husky, brawling laughter of
  Youth, half-naked, sweating, proud to be Hog
  Butcher, Tool Maker, Stacker of Wheat, Player with
  Railroads and Freight Handler to the Nation.

"Chicago"

Directions: Select one of the following options. ▲

> Create a collage of photos that shows Chicago during the time period this poem was written.

> Make a poster that shares information about Carl Sandburg.

> Make a set of concentration cards to match at least 10 vocabulary words from the poem with their definitions.

- -

"Chicago"

Directions: Select one of the following options. ●

> Make an acrostic for the name of your town with specific descriptions for each letter.

> Consider your town as it was 100 years ago. Make a Venn diagram to compare and contrast it then and now.

> Write a three facts and a fib about Chicago based on Sandburg's poem.

- -

"Chicago"

Directions: Select one of the following options. ■

> Read at least one more poem by Carl Sandburg. Make a PowerPoint in which you analyze the poems and draw conclusions about his writing style.

> Write an original poem about where you live using a style similar to Sandburg's.

> Record a commercial to promote your town; be sure to share both its faults and virtues.

"I, Too, Sing America"

Poetry Shape Menu

Reading Objectives Covered Through This Menu and These Activities

- Students will compare one literary work with another.
- Students will interpret figurative language and multiple meaning words.
- Students will make predictions based on what is read.
- Students will use resources and references to build meaning.

Writing Objectives Covered Through This Menu and These Activities

- Students will write to express their feelings, reflect, inform, explain, describe, or narrate.
- Students will use vivid language.
- Students will exhibit voice in their writing.

Materials Needed by Students for Completion

- "I, Too, Sing America" by Langston Hughes
- Poster board or large white paper
- Microsoft PowerPoint or other slideshow software ●
- DVD or VHS recorder (for documentaries, news reports) ■

Special Notes on the Modifications of This Menu

- This menu is unique from the others, as teachers can select the number of choices based on the amount of time they plan to spend processing a particular poem. This menu is divided into three sections, the top ▲ or triangle section has activities with the most modifications, the middle ● or circle section has activities with minor modifications, and the lower ■ or square section has activities that offer the most extension. If the goal is to have students create one product for the poem, then the teacher can provide each student with a strip of an appropriate level of options. For a more in-depth study, the teacher can provide the entire menu and students select one option from each section of the menu.

Special Notes on the Use of This Menu

- The square strip of the menu ■ gives students the opportunity to create a documentaries and news reports. Although students enjoy producing their own videos, there often are difficulties obtaining the equipment and scheduling the use of a video recorder. This activity can be modified by allowing students to act out the product (like a play) or, if students have the technology, allowing them to produce a webcam version of their product.

Time Frame

- 1 week—Students are given the menu before the poem is read. The teacher will go over all of the options for the menu and have students indicate each option that represents the activity they are most interested in completing. The teacher may assign the menu as independent work or choose to allow students time to work after their other work is finished.
- 1–2 days—The teacher chooses a strip for each student to complete based on his or her specific needs. The student selects one of the activities on the strip and works on it for independent practice.

Suggested Forms

- All-purpose rubric
- Student presentation rubric
- Free-choice proposal form

"I, Too, Sing America"

Directions: Select one of the following options. ▲

Write a paragraph to summarize this poem and its meaning.

Free choice: Submit your free choice proposal to your teacher for approval.

Retell the meaning of the poem using your own words.

"I, Too, Sing America"

Directions: Select one of the following options. ●

Pretend you could interview the narrator of this poem. Write the questions you would ask and provide reasonable responses.

Prepare a PowerPoint presentation that shares historical events that explain the meaning of this poem.

Compose a letter that the narrator could write to America concerning his feelings.

"I, Too, Sing America"

Directions: Select one of the following options. ■

Select two poems by other authors that could be companions for this poem. Record a documentary in which you read all of the poems and explain their importance.

Would the narrator still feel the same way in present day? Prepare a speech that the narrator might give to share his or her feelings about present-day America.

Record an original news report in which the newscaster uses this poem to accompany a report of a current (national or international) event.

The Book of Questions

Poetry Shape Menu

The Book of Questions contains 74 different poems by Pablo Neruda, and different teachers may have access to different poems from the book. Therefore, this menu has been designed in such a way that it can used with any number of the poems from *The Book of Questions*.

Reading Objectives Covered Through This Menu and These Activities

- Students will compare one literary work with another.
- Students will interpret figurative language and multiple meaning words.
- Students will make predictions based on what is read.
- Students will use resources and references to build meaning.

Writing Objectives Covered Through This Menu and These Activities

- Students will write to express their feelings, reflect, inform, explain, describe, or narrate.
- Students will use vivid language.
- Students will exhibit voice in their writing.

Materials Needed by Students for Completion

- Poems taken from *The Book of Questions* by Pedro Neruda
- Poster board or large white paper
- *The Book of Questions* cube template ●
- DVD or VHS recorder (for commercials, videos) ■

Special Notes on the Modifications of This Menu

- This menu is unique from the others, as teachers can select the number of choices based on the amount of time they plan to spend processing a particular poem. This menu is divided into three sections, the top ▲ or triangle section has activities with the most modifications, the middle ● or circle section has activities with minor modifications, and the lower ■ or square section has activities that offer the most extension. If the goal is to have students create one product for the poem, then the teacher can provide each student with a strip of an appropriate level of options. For a more in-depth study, the teacher can provide the entire menu and students select one option from each section of the menu.

Special Notes on the Use of This Menu

- The square strip of the menu ■ gives students the opportunity to create a video or commercial. Although students enjoy producing their own videos, there often are difficulties obtaining the equipment and scheduling the use of a video recorder. This activity can be modified by allowing students to act out the product (like a play) or, if students have the technology, allowing them to produce a webcam version of their product.

Time Frame

- 1 week—Students are given the menu before the poem is read. The teacher will go over all of the options for the menu and have students indicate each option that represents the activity they are most interested in completing. The teacher may assign the menu as independent work or choose to allow students time to work after their other work is finished.
- 1–2 days—The teacher chooses a strip for each student to complete based on his or her specific needs. The student selects one of the activities on the strip and works on it for independent practice.

Suggested Forms

- All-purpose rubric
- Student presentation rubric

Name: _____

The Book of Questions

Directions: Select one of the following options.   ▲

Make a mind map
to organize all of
the questions found
in the poem.

Create a poster for
one of the questions
in the poem. Your
poster should have
an illustration to
accompany the
question you selected.

Make a Venn diagram
to compare the types of
questions found in two
of Neruda's poems.

- -

The Book of Questions

Directions: Select one of the following options.   ●

Write an original
poem answering
all of the questions
posed by one of Pablo
Neruda's poems.

Complete *The Book
of Questions* cube.

Make an acrostic for
the word *question*.
Write an interesting
question for each letter.

- -

The Book of Questions

Directions: Select one of the following options.   ■

Create your own
question poem using a
format similar to a *Book
of Questions* poem.

Create a commercial in
which you use questions
to convince someone
to buy a product.

Record a video in which
you share a video poem
made from questions
you have always
pondered about the
world around you.

The Book of Questions Cube

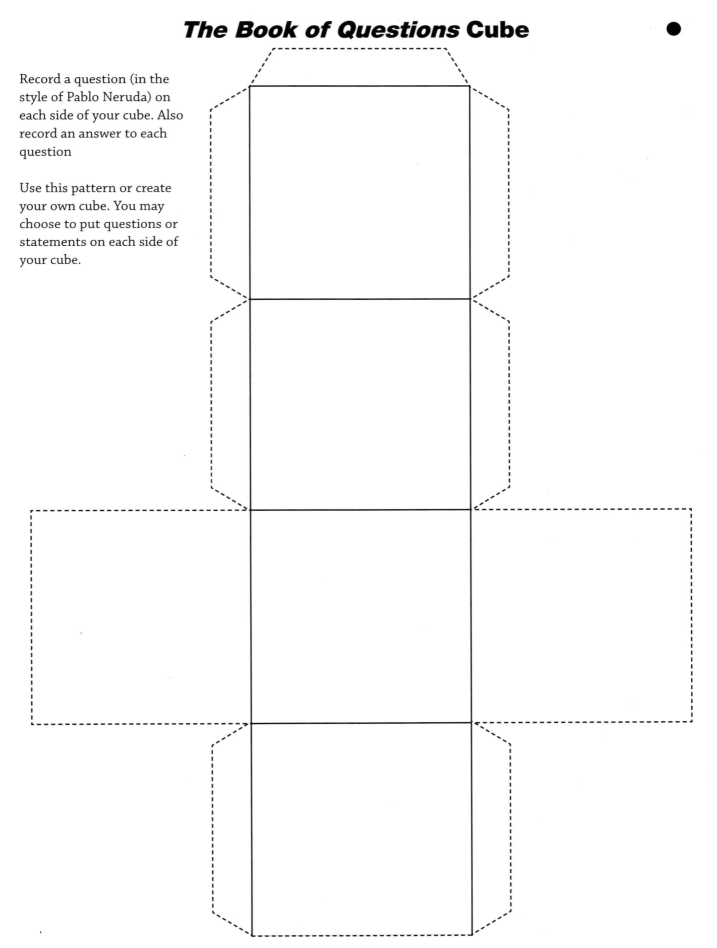

Record a question (in the style of Pablo Neruda) on each side of your cube. Also record an answer to each question

Use this pattern or create your own cube. You may choose to put questions or statements on each side of your cube.

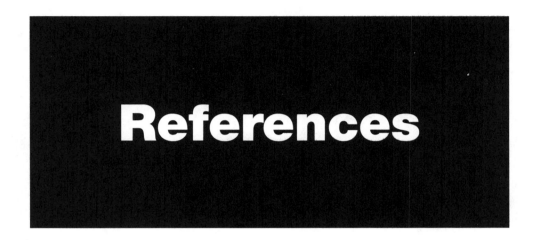

References

Anderson, L. W., & Krathwohl, D. R. (Eds.). (2001). *A taxonomy for learning, teaching, and assessing: A revision of Bloom's taxonomy of educational objectives.* New York, NY: Allyn & Bacon.

Cipani, E. (1995). Inclusive education: What do we know and what do we still have to learn? *Exceptional Children, 61,* 498–500.

Keen, D. (2001). *Talent in the new millennium: A two-year research study of gifted education.* Retrieved from http://files.eric.ed.gov/fulltext/EJ854972.pdf

About the Author

After teaching science for more than 15 years, both overseas and in the U.S., **Laurie E. Westphal** now works as an independent gifted education and science consultant nationwide. She enjoys developing and presenting staff development on differentiation for various districts and conferences, working with teachers to assist them in planning and developing lessons to meet the needs of all students. Laurie currently resides in Houston, TX, and has made it her goal to convert as many teachers as she can to the differentiated lifestyle in the classroom and share her vision for real-world, product-based lessons that help all students become critical thinkers and effective problem solvers.

If you are interested in having Laurie speak at your next staff development day or conference, please visit her website, http://www.giftedconsultant.com, for additional information.

Common Core State Standards Alignment

This book aligns with an extensive number of the Common Core State Standards for ELA-Literacy. Please visit http://www.prufrock.com/ccss to download a complete packet of the standards that align with each individual menu in this book.